The Reasoning behind *the* Act *of* Striking *a* Spent Match

Other books by Hernán Fontanet

Al sur de casi todo. Humberto Costantini y su obra.

In Praise of Tears: The Quest for Identity in Humberto Costantini's Poetry

Gelman: Un poeta y su vida

Juan Gelman y su tiempo: Historias, poemas y reflexiones

The Unfinished Song of Francisco Urondo: When Poetry is Not Enough

Francisco Urondo y su poesía: un arma cargada de futuro

Modelo y su(b)versión en la poética de Leónidas Lamborghini

Fervor y exilio en la poética de Humberto Costantini

Poéticas de exilio

The Reasoning behind *the* Act *of* Striking *a* Spent Match

The Poetry of Juan Gelman

Hernán Fontanet

TCU Press

Fort Worth, Texas

Library of Congress Cataloging-in-Publication Data

Names: Fontanet, Hernán, author.
Title: The reasoning behind the act of striking a spent match : the poetry of Juan Gelman / Hernán Fontanet.
Description: Fort Worth, Texas : TCU Press, [2019] | Includes bibliographical references.
Identifiers: LCCN 2019011579 | ISBN 9780875657141 (alk. paper)
Subjects: LCSH: Gelman, Juan, 1930-2014--Criticism and interpretation. | Political poetry, Argentine--20th century--History and criticism. | Exiles' writings, Argentine--20th century--History and criticism.
Classification: LCC PQ7797.G386 Z6744 2019 | DDC 861/.64--dc23
LC record available at https://urldefense.proofpoint.com/v2/url?u=https-3A__lccn.loc.gov_2019011579&d=DwIF-g&c=7Q-FWLBTAxn3T_E3HWrzGYJrC4RvUoWDrzTlitGRH_A&r=O2eiy819IcwTGuw-vrBGiVdmhQxMh2yxeggw9qlTUDE&m=mwrnxb5fGz080oIC_qTBfu_Ea9Nu7IO8PzgHBWTwfD8&s=npnkdJXG_1-mFzYfC4BHmAM6WOu2iqT5aJxB12CBHmQ&e=

TCU Press

TCU Box 298300
Fort Worth, Texas 76129
817.257.7822
www.prs.tcu.edu
To order books: 1.800.826.8911

Design by John Barnett | 4eyesdesign.com

Contents

Foreword

A Complete and Profound Analysis

As one of the truly great poets of my generation, Juan Gelman's reputation is admirably served by this thoughtful, deeply intelligent analysis of his life and work. Gelman was the consummate poet—one who had an almost miraculous ability to voice not only his own fears, hopes, and dreams but also those of an era. He believed that poetry was his life's tutor; it taught him how to walk and how be truly *human* in the deepest sense of the word.

I speak from experience: Juan Gelman was my friend from my youth. We experienced life and injustice together. Our hearts and minds were bound by the shared sadness of the oppressed—serving time in jail together and living under death threats from those in power. Together, we wrote *Exilio* to tell the story of the injustice that plagued so many—some who simply disappeared, no doubt to die obscure deaths out of sight, out of mind. But Juan had the gift of using his poetry to expose these atrocities—"Not alive nor dead," the dictator would say in front of the screen. And Juan, with poetry in hand, will leave it exposed forever; naked but with uniform; naked with a hat of officers of obscure death. His poems were like a dagger in that night without dawn.

In this book, *The Reasoning behind the Act of Striking a Spent Match: The Poetry of Juan Gelman*, Hernán Fontanet portrays his subject masterfully and truthfully, poignantly framing Gelman's poetry, his landscape, and his mind. Previously, I had the pleasure of writing a prologue to another biographical work written by Fontanet, *The Unfinished Song of Francisco Urondo: When Poetry is Not Enough*. In this book, Fontanet analyzes the life of poet Francisco "Paco" Urondo and delves into the man behind the literature with equal talent.

In this new biography, Hernán Fontanet captures the spirit and essence of Juan Gelman, the poet, and immerses himself in the broad sweep of Juan's poetry, giving the reader not just a painstaking literary analysis but also deep insight into the life and person of Juan Gelman. Through Fontanet's analysis, we delve into Juan's life experiences and begin to see how persecution and isolation fed his imagination and creativity with exquisite images that grew more intricate with each experience. Capturing the poet's involvements with unmatched literary beauty, Fontanet presents us with a unique poet—someone with a creative mind who lived on the edge.

As Juan's friend, I can say that Fontanet's portrayal of Juan is accurate—this is how he was. He never abandoned complicated situations—always searching for humanity despite so much conflict and death. He expressed his search emphatically in the words of his poetry. I am thankful that the details of his practices and understandings have been so accurately captured here.

In this volume, Hernán Fontanet helps the reader gain insights into his poetry by first understanding more about the poet himself. Fontanet presents Gelman in relief against the backdrop of his hopes and dreams, his fantasies, and the courage he displayed in the face of great cruelty. Juan Gelman becomes more human with every verse analyzed in the book. Fontanet's truthful portrayal brought Gelman from a brilliant but ambiguous poet, to a living, breathing being struggling to search for a new path and new words. In this analysis Juan Gelman grows in stature, not as a vigilant marble giant but as a passionate human being who searched for a new path and new words. His "new" words inspired others to dream and envision new paths and to continue the search nonstop. This relentless search is what Juan Gelman achieved with his poetry. In fact, it was this very uncompromising curiosity that ignited Juan Gelman's masterful poetry. In his life, he didn't achieve personal comfort, but he dreamed of possibilities far beyond his own reality.

Fontanet has created a grand tribute for Gelman, using his favorite weapon—his poetry. Reading Gelman, through this complete work, is to enter into the life of a great poet.

—*Osvaldo Bayer*

Osvaldo Bayer is an Argentinian writer, historian, journalist, and human rights activist best known for his highly acclaimed book *La Patagonia Rebelde* (*Rebellion in Patagonia*). He was born on February 18, 1927, in Santa Fe, Argentina, where his family had immigrated from Altenburg, Germany.

In *La Patagonia Rebelde*, Bayer recounts the early 1920s strike of rural Patagonian workers who were cruelly repressed by the military under the Hipólito Yrigoyen government. Among Bayer's other important works are *Severino Di Giovanni, el Idealista de la violencia, The Anarchist Expropriators*, and the fictional novel *Rainer and Minou*. As a screenwriter, he participated in the *La Patagonia Rebelde* film which was directed by Héctor Olivera and won a Silver Berlin Bear at the Berlin International Film Festival in 1974.

During the Dirty War, Bayer was subject to constant death threats, and his books were publicly banned. Many of his friends, including the writer Rodolfo Walsh and the poet Francisco Urondo, were kidnapped and murdered. In 1975, Bayer managed to escape from Argentina with the help of the West German embassy.

He returned a week before the fall of the military dictatorship. He went on to write for *Página/12* and was an instructor at the German Development Foundation in Bad Honnef. Bayer received the title of *Doctor Honoris Causa* from the national universities of Comahue (1999), San Luis (2006), Del Sur (2007), Córdoba (2009), Quilmes (2009), and San Juan (2011).

Introduction

In 1976, at two o'clock one winter morning, paramilitary forces broke into a house in a quiet upscale neighborhood of Buenos Aires. Inside, sleeping, were two nineteen-year-old girls and a twenty-year-old boy. This was the house of the esteemed Argentinian poet Juan Gelman, but he was not home. Frustrated, the soldiers kidnapped the three young people—Gelman's daughter, son, and seven-months-pregnant daughter-in-law. They disappeared into the night. In 1990, Gelman found out that his son had been executed and his remains buried in a barrel filled with sand and cement. Ten years later he was able to locate his granddaughter, who had been born in a back-alley hospital and given to a pro-government family.

For Juan Gelman, one of the most celebrated Latin American poets of the twentieth century, that night was one of many close calls. Born in 1930, his was a life of narrow escapes. As an Ashkenazi Jew poet, guerrilla fighter, freethinker, and prolific journalist, he escaped three death sentences decreed by groups on both the right and the left in Argentina. He was a victim of state terrorism in that country, and still he let his voice be heard.

For his poetry, Juan Gelman was awarded the Miguel de Cervantes Prize in 2007, the most prestigious award in Spanish literature. Because nothing could suppress his voice, he found expression for the dream of an entire generation. Gelman died in 2014. His life was fraught with torture and loss. The turbulent history of his country, as well as of the entire region, changed forever his way of looking at the world.

What Does Gelman's Work Discuss?

The core themes of Juan Gelman's work seem to vary throughout his diverse collection and evolve to incorporate his current situation; however, death and nothingness, the existential questions, are tropes that appear often, especially toward the end of his life. More traditional literary considerations highlight other concerns present in Gelman's work, such as the question about the nature of poetry, the inclusion of multiple voices through the use of pseudonyms, as well as three poignant themes shaping his work: exile, identity, and otherness.

Gelman was a rover who lived in more than twenty cities during his thirteen-year-long exile. While his exile ended in 1988, the effect it had on him endured and left an indelible mark on his poetry.

During his exile, he spoke at length about his own identity, which he found to be in a permanent state of conflict. Gelman discussed how the stigma of being the first Argentinian in his family, in addition to all the time he spent in exile, weighed on him. Gelman had many competing and intersecting identities, and these had an obvious effect on his work. He was Ukrainian, Argentinian, and Mexican, as well as an Ashkenazi Christian Jew who wrote in Sephardi and Argentinian (River Plate) Spanish. As a child he listened to Russian literature, Ukrainian speech, and Hebrew theater. This diverse and eclectic background formed his views.

The third theme identified by critics, otherness, arose from a political and militant mindset that sprang from Gelman's continuous denouncement of the exclusion of minority groups. Gelman was cognizant of how biases led to certain groups of people being politically, geographically, and intellectually excluded from hegemonic historiography. Through his work, the poet tried to restore millions of voices—the voices of those described as "nobodies" in Eduardo Galeano's works, termed "subalterns" by Antonio Gramsci, and depicted as the "Juanitos Laguna" in Antonio Berni's paintings. These socially invisible, second-class citizens comprise the chorus of voices that populate Gelman's works. They are the voices that emerge from the fringes of social classes, the barefooted pariahs who walk along the muddy edges of the world and soak their feet, for example, in the neoclassical water fountains of Buenos Aires, immortalized in the poetry of Leónidas Lamborghini. They are those fallen-off-the-map, unregistered people who are "worth less than the bullet that kills them."[1] They are the "Pepe Díaz," "María the Maid," and "Pedro the Bricklayer" in the pages of Gelman's writings. The "others" that Gelman portrays in his works are also the artists, poets, and social activists who have worked tirelessly to change the status quo in their respective societies. They include Rodolfo Walsh, García Lorca, Attila József, "Paco" Urondo, Patrice Lumumba, Jiří Wolker, the Mothers of Plaza de Mayo, and many other less well-known and less frequently discussed figures.

In addition to the main themes in Gelman's work already mentioned (death, nothingness, poetry, pseudonyms, exile, identity, and otherness), it is possible to posit a transcendent reading that unites these and other issues in a perspective combining two primordial concepts: language and power. Gelman's greatest strategic and poetic actions as a writer occur amid the ongoing tension between power and language.

Gelman and Postcolonial Theory

The themes that constitute Gelman's identity (exile, otherness, and language), which are also the conceptual core of postcolonial literature, are reflected as well in Gelman's political activity.

Postcolonialism, which has been influenced by many postmodern schools of thought, offers methods of analysis and interpretation for understanding the effects and implications of neocolonialism and servitude.

The most important assumptions utilized by the great theorists in this vein—such as Palestinian American critic Edward Saïd; Kenyan dramaturge Ngũgĩ wa Thiong'o; Indian philosopher Gayatri Chakravorty Spivak, who wrote the celebrated *Can the Subaltern Speak?*; and Martinique-born Afro-Caribbean psychiatrist Frantz Fanon—focus on the analysis of a dominant discourse creating our notion of "reality."

This grandiose discourse, built over hundreds of years and designed to serve the ethnocentric perspectives and value systems of the rulers of the moment, divides people into two groups. This dividing mechanism creates the identity of the system's winners, as well as that of its "others," those nonwinners who are quickly disposed of or exiled if they disobey the "laws of [this discourse-created] reality."[2]

In other words, whereas history embalms the words of the victorious and passes them honorably across generations, it quickly incinerates the words of the defeated, not even bothering to sift through those words for such true and useful insights as they might contain. The reigning metanarrative (of which history is an expression) attempts to control and nullify any form of autonomous, independent, and self-managed rhetoric that conflicts with official discourse. Its goal is to convince the multitudes that their interests coincide with those of the elites. The masses, Gelman believed, are squeezed by the mighty few into virtual concentration camps to be regularly gassed with propaganda and rigidly bent by the subjective opinions of the established elites.

In his work, Gelman boldly challenged this structure, attempting to ventilate a civic atmosphere choked with suppression, prejudice, and fear. Gelman's work can be interpreted as a great literary effort to create a countercultural alternative to the official story being spread by those in power. As a postcolonial writer, Gelman downplayed the notion of "absolute truth" that dictates the way the world works today.

Disputing Semantics

Gelman understood that his exile was just part of a larger, ongoing intellectual and ideological dispute—a dispute that was not territorial, like the big wars in years past, but very much ideological and even semantic; a war waged not in trenches but in the mind, one waged with sophisticated artillery hidden in language. He realized that those who create the narrative will hold the power; those who give us our understanding of how the world works will impose their perspective and opinions onto the world. Gelman thought of democracy as an entelechy that was gradually fading away, leaving in its place the ashes of a paradisal equality. He recognized the existence of a hegemonic ethnocentric force shaping the way we see the world, a force that establishes parameters around racial, linguistic, religious, and social categories. But he also discovered a powerful countercultural effort working to break down these parameters.

Gelman's work reflects his belief in the power of words and shows how tensions arise when conflicting interests use words for their own purposes.

From the early stages of his analysis, Gelman assumed that the physicality of the word is the field of fierce battles; that conflicting interests drag words from one place to another, forcing preferred interpretations upon them so that they will say what these interests want to be heard, and so that any inconvenient truths they might otherwise communicate will be silenced. Historiographies, he felt, soften the sharp and threatening content of some words in order to shape and influence our thinking.

The word, as a commodity, has always been at the center of debate. Behind the polished diplomacy in which the world is fashionably dressed, there rage ferocious battles fought in semantic trenches. For example, the "sheep" to which the shepherd refers is called "lamb" on the table of the feudal lord; the "beef" the wealthy person eats is nothing more than the humble "cow" raised by the rural peasant. Linguistic disagreement mirrors social tensions and class struggle. Words reflect a linguistic tussle reminiscent of the social fractures dividing societies. The farmer undersells the "pig" served as "pork" on the banker's plate. Indigenous people fatten the "cock" and "hen" that the conqueror calls "chicken." Words reveal a source. In the minds of listeners, words determine speakers' places of origin, different levels of knowledge, and social statuses. Fierce combat over nomenclature rages among classes of the society.

In the verbal sphere, battles for power occur. In the verbal struggle, power imposes its harshness on words. Those words reproduce that dominance. Official history ennobles the words of the victorious. Those of the losers are tossed aside, their value subordinated and undermined.

Perhaps the most important contribution of Gelman's work to the symphony of contemporary literature concerns the relentless search for the right word, a word that skips the preset script and appeals to that which opposes a single way of thinking. Gelman realized that the precise word is subversive: if we find the right term, and with it succeed in cutting through the communicative encirclement put in place around us by a network of linguistic operations, we will have taken a great step toward linguistic emancipation, toward sovereign and revolutionary communication.

It is possible, Gelman believed, to recover the libertarian, unrestricted, and untamed word. The veracious word can, he recognized, rename the poorly christened, deny tales of greed, remove the dirt of apathy and indulgence, and climb the towers of royal academies, taking them by assault in the manner of storming fortresses, or *Bastilles*. The magical glow of invention and adventure *can* be returned to words—such was Gelman's conviction. Making this possibility a reality was his task and main purpose, and he dedicated his eighty-three years of life to this end.

Gelman's work challenges power, accuses it, and interprets it, without trying to elude the gesture of doubt, definitely the most formidable guardian of intellectual honesty. His work rebels against the linguistic establishment, and such rebellion became the main theme of Gelman's career. By standing up to the tendentiously stagnant word, Gelman's work seeks to subvert that which rules and objectifies us.

That is why Gelman, to fashion his poetry, needed to create new words, regulate irregular verbs, masculinize feminine nouns, feminize male adjectives, and engage in dialogue with poetic materials written half a millennium ago. The most notorious aspect of Gelman's work is his untiring archaeological expeditions into buried diction. Through such expeditions, Gelman tried to excavate the correct words, the words best able to contravene dogmatic vocabulary, often discovering that the precise word needed was hidden away under a metallic crust of societal bias forged by calculating linguistic blacksmiths. He campaigned for verbal liberation with words unshackled from canon. Refusing to reverence the institutions of language, and looking inquisitively into their unlighted closets, he pushed to unearth buried words, to restore the muscularity of rickety words, and to rub the mind with immortal poetry. He wanted to bring back to words the daring edges incorrectly hidden away in linguistic courtesy; he searched for a "lost innocence" and for a fresh beginning because he understood that the powerful burning that warms the renewed word cannot be quenched—not by a hurricane of dollars nor by the fiercest oppression.

For this reason, we have chosen the title of this book. We have chosen it because Gelman never accepted that a burned match cannot be relit; because he believed in the mystery of the unknown and unfathomable, in our infinite ignorance, in the force of the countercurrent, in the power of the useless act; because he believed in revisiting, recreating, and igniting what for most people is exhausted, nonexistent, or dead—because, in short, he believed in the all-is-possible of poetry.

No matter how monstrous the faces of the hegemonic power were, Gelman—Communist at fifteen and Montonero[3] at thirty—confronted them with reason and utopias.

It did not matter with what tools he chose to undertake the attack. At first, he tried with weapons, and he failed miserably. After that, he continued the fight on the terrain of liberated language, and there he continued to battle.

It also did not matter how immature ("*inberbes*") were the Montoneros, how tyrannical and restrictive were the hendecasyllables, or how bloody were the Ford Falcons of the Marine Corps; Gelman confronted them and unraveled their verbal strategies. None of these battles were excluded from his poetry. With his personal writing and his peculiar form, which makes you travel through his reality, all his fighting conformed to the unique unity of his life.

The Time and Place of Juan Gelman's Life

The life and work of Juan Gelman are both disturbing and poignant. Gelman's fate was marked since he was a child with personal tragedy, political and religious persecution, and mourning.

Gelman's Ukrainian grandparents were persecuted for being Jewish, suffering attacks and pogroms that were also endured by family and friends. One of Gelman's aunts died in a fire set by Cossacks and Eastern European, anti-Semitic groups. His father survived abuse and mistreatment at the hands of the Tsarist police and was forced to escape Russia and flee to Argentina. This journey resulted in the death of his first wife and their son, Gelman's half brother.

Gelman's descendants did not suffer any less. Both of his children were kidnapped, and one was assassinated in cold blood. His daughter-in-law was apprehended and, to this day, remains missing as a *desaparecida*. His baby granddaughter was seized and "raised in captivity," unaware of her true identity for over twenty-three years.

Clearly, Gelman followed in his father's footsteps. Gelman also suffered terrorist-state harassment and dictator-led persecution. The Argentinean military dictatorship—inspired by American McCarthyism, anti-Semitism, and the xenophobia of Nazi Germany—pursued, kidnapped, tortured, declared missing, or assassinated Gelman's friends and family. If any still live, their whereabouts are unknown; and of those who are dead, there exist neither traces of their remains nor tombstones at which to mourn them. The search for many of them continues to this day.

When repeated death threats forced Gelman into exile, just as his father had been forced into exile fifty years earlier, silence and solitude dominated his existence, which had a profoundly stifling effect on his work. Gelman found it impossible to write and create for many years.

Owing to a formidable survival instinct, however, Gelman rose above the numerous adverse circumstances that confronted him. Through courage and conviction, he was able to reshape many aspects of his life, and his legacy has endured.

Despite the countless personal tragedies that he suffered, his final days were filled with love and contentment. One of the great lessons we learn when we read Gelman's poetry is expressed by the words of another poet, Mario Benedetti, when he mentions the need of "Defending joy as if it were a trench," even in the most atrocious circumstances. In the face of the torment of the Argentinian military prisons, Gelman unleashed the powerful weapon of his poetry, with which he managed to overcome pessimism and decipher the secret code of acceptance and joy.

Gelman's life was an example of strength, determination, and positivity. His political ideals, coupled with a passion for poetry and journalism, filled him with the glowing spark of life. With this foundation, he learned to create a strategy that enabled him to cope with endless tragedies. By combining art with a demand for justice and literary creation with social criticism, Gelman was able to forge his ultimately powerful image.

His biography and literary legacy have permanently raised the flag of memory, helping to ensure that this type of tragedy is not repeated. His definitive work will survive with the dignity his accomplishments deserve.

Gelman's extensive body of work, consisting of a literary career spanning over sixty years, is distinctive and many years ahead of his contemporaries. His work followed a path that began like that of many other talented poets of the 1950s. Gradually it evolved into a singular, more powerful and impregnable voice, one that was tempered and refined over a life span of eighty-plus years.

Gelman's unique voice paved a clear path through the confusing panorama of contemporary letters. His was a voice that demonstrated wisdom, relying upon a life lived to corroborate each word. This voice did not arise of out of sudden inspiration; rather, it was the product of deliberate, sustained expression, careful discernment, and a lengthy period of ripening.

His work unfolds like a multicolored fan, extending the nuances and harmonies of his dreams. This work is written in a state of permanent zeal, as the idea is expressed in one of his poems. Gelman was the creator of small linguistic wonders that no condition or event could ever suppress—not dictatorships, not bureaucratic entities, not even the frustration and solitude that his own success could not prevail over. His poetry represents a free reflection sprung forth from a creative word, a thought that encompasses the dream of an entire generation. Gelman's words are active and born of action: irrepressible, undefeatable, and redeeming.

More than the writing of many poets, Gelman's work is the story of his life. His poetry added definition to the previously indefinable, going beyond the boundaries designated by dictionaries and academics. As a result, his life was, and his works are, genuine and distinctive.

This book aims to encompass the physical, familiar, intellectual, and political environment of the time and space of Juan Gelman's life. The poet's time on earth, as well as his more than thirty books, are carefully examined, and the course of his whole existence dissected, struggle by struggle and verse by verse. From one belief to another that is stronger, through historical events and tragedies, the journey culminates in a revelation of the music and landscape of his life in his verses.

Every great writer is greater than his own life and literary works. With this criterion in mind, we have assembled this book, where themes, recurrences, exiles, terrible stories, longings, fears, and hope appear. This explains why we have selected different aspects of Gelman's life and work, without focusing too much on chronology, knowing that Gelman's poetry and experiences are inexhaustible and not bound by any restrictive canons.

This book attempts to pass along the energy, pleasure, pity, astonishment, and love for poetry that we experience each time we enter Gelman's universe.

On behalf of poetic and social justice, for the distribution of knowledge and wealth, so that more may benefit for the benefit of all, the struggle to control history's narrative will never stop.

Welcome, reader, to this binding of riotous pages.

The Foreigners. Family Portrait I

José Emilio Pacheco Berny, a Mexican poet, personal friend of Gelman, and recipient of the Miguel de Cervantes Prize, the most prestigious and remunerative award given for Spanish-language literature, describes the political and cultural context in which the poet was born as follows:

> He came into the world six months after Wall Street collapsed and marked the beginning of the big recession that history recognized as the Great Depression. His contemporaries were the painter Jasper Johns; filmmaker Clint Eastwood; Sean Connery; Neil Armstrong, the first astronaut to walk on the moon; Harold Pinter; Jean-Luc Godard; and Jean-Louis Trintignant. In the film *Blue Angel*, Marlene Dietrich emerged as a great star. . . . The books of the year were *My Life: An Attempt at an Autobiography* by Leon Trotsky; *Civilization and Its Discontents* by Sigmund Freud; and two novels that continue to be read, *As I Lay Dying* by William Faulkner and *The Maltese Falcon* by Dashiell Hammett. On their path to power, Hitler's followers stoned the Jewish stores in Berlin…
> . . . Sir Arthur Conan Doyle, Ana Pavlova, and D. H. Lawrence died. Stalin justified the purge of 6,500 members of the Communist party for allegedly being supporters of Trotsky.[4]

The morning of May 3, 1930, at 11:00 a.m., Juan Gelman was born in the Durand Hospital, in the city of Buenos Aires, Argentina, under the zodiac sign of Taurus. His family, including at that time his father Joseph (known as José in Argentina), his mother Paulina, his oldest brother Boris, and his sister Teodora, welcomed their first Argentine member. The family's other members had been born in Ukraine and Moscow of Jewish descent and had arrived in Buenos Aires a few years earlier, fleeing the tragedy and failure that so often plagues human beings.

Periods of great capitalist expansion are usually followed by economic crises, social inequalities, usury, massive migrations, and monstrous world wars, for which the vulnerable sectors pay the greatest price. After the industrial and commercial booms at the end of the nineteenth and beginning of the twentieth century, the financial crisis of 1929 occurred between two world wars—that, in reality, were one large and violent conflict interrupted by a brief interval of peace.

Although the peripheral and emergent condition of Latin America meant that it did not intervene actively in any of the sustained conflicts, this period still had dire consequences for the region. These included speculation in raw materials and unequal commerce. The consequences were indebtedness, poverty, and underdevelopment.

In an attempt to oppose the tyranny of capital, with its restrictive economic plans and the havoc that caused usury, revolutionary ideas arose along with the revulsive and insurgent art of the vanguards. In this way, the avant-garde, purified and essential, inaugurated a new chapter in the story of art and in contemporary thought.

The years between 1920 and 1940 were particularly intense for citizens of the Western world. It was into this hopelessly complex and paradoxical environment of full expectations that Juan Gelman Burichson was born in Buenos Aires.

In a report of journalist Rodolfo Braceli that appeared in the newspaper *La Nación* of Buenos Aires in 2010, Gelman recalled the first sensations when he was born:

> —Tell me about your birth, did you collaborate or did you just sit there?
> —I collaborated. When my mom gave birth to me, I wanted to be next to her. That's the least that a gentleman can do.
> —Do you remember being born?

—Of course! What it cost me! It seems like my mother was fine with me and didn't want to let me out. I went through twenty-six hours of what you call hard labor, until, fighting a little, I got out weighing 5.5 kilograms. They called me the bull of the room. According to my mom, a nun tried to steal me.

—Really, a nun?

—I believe it's something that belongs to the family's legend.[5]

His Father

Joseph Gelman, Juan's father, was born in 1890. He was a carpenter in his native Ukraine and came from a humble Jewish family. Juan inherited two passions from him: love for literature and political commitment.

According to Gelman, his dad was a voracious reader, "One of those laborers of Russia's revolutionary generation who knew everything: economy, history, and political science. Now you would call this person wise."[6]

A product of social and political revolutionary affiliation, Joseph Gelman actively participated in the 1905 revolution against the monarchy of Czar Nicholas II of Russia. After the revolt failed, a time of deception and paranoia arrived. Consequently, he was forced to search for a refuge before deciding to run away.

> I didn't know of the revolutionary activity of my father until much later in 1957, when I encountered my two aunts and cousin in Moscow. They still lived in the wooden house where he had found refuge, and from where he escaped because the Czar's police were right behind him. Later, he wandered to other regions of Russia, God knows where . . .[7]

With a fake passport in hand, Joseph Gelman decided to embark to the Americas, the Promised Land. He set off alone for Genoa, leaving his family behind. At that point, the family consisted of his first wife and two sons. Once he arrived at the Italian city, Joseph Gelman had to decide between two possible destinations: Buenos Aires or New York. The selection was not complicated. With the czarist police right behind him and with precarious documentation, he chose the ship with a Buenos Aires destination—it was the first ship to sail.

In 1912, once he arrived in the capital of Argentina, he found a job as a railroad worker in the city of Campana. Years later, enthusiastic over the triumph of the Russian Revolution of 1917, he tried to return to Ukraine to be reunited with his family. However, the Ukrainian authorities tried to stop him. There was great instability on the borders—one of the consequences of the continuous attacks of the European monarchies, which were attempting to stop the anti-monarchy and anti-capitalist revolution at any cost. It was estimated that up to eighteen battle fronts had been opened by capitalist powers seeking to defeat the Russian Revolution by hazing the recently triumphant Red Army (Krasnaya Armiya).

Once in Ukraine, he was disappointed by the changing course of events. Above all, he was disenchanted about having provided his support for the rise of Joseph Stalin within the Communist Party structure. Considering the subsequent expulsion of Leon Trotsky, whom he admired, he opted to abandon indefinitely what had become the Soviet Union and travel with his wife and sons a second time to Buenos Aires. Gelman described that moment:

> Although he wasn't completely a Trotskyite, he admired Trotsky and thought that, with his departure from the scene, the last possibility for a democratic debate in the Soviet Unions had vanished.[8]

Their escape plan failed tragically when they tried to get away by crossing a river. Joseph's wife and youngest son fell into the water and drowned. In an interview, Juan Gelman recounted the painful episode as follows:

> José [Joseph] Gelman made all the arrangements to cross a river and escape on a small boat. But in the middle of the passage, the boat turned, and his wife and youngest son drowned to death. Boris [the older son] was saved because a soldier jumped into the water and got him out by his hair.[9]

Juan was unaware of the existence of his deceased brother until 2000. When he was seventy, the widow of his half-brother Boris revealed to him what had occurred. He would never know his drowned brother's name:

> So, I recovered a dead brother, a thousand years after he was gone. Stories that happen in most families, areas that you don't touch. . . . I don't know, the family's secret is always roaming around. . . . [10]

This unhappy event delayed a definite trip to Buenos Aires for years. In the meantime, Joseph Gelman and his only son, Boris, ended up meeting a Jewish medical student, Paulina Burichson, in Odessa. Joseph and Paulina married after a brief, sentimental relationship and decided to go to Argentina together. Juan Gelman described those years as follows:

> They had a daughter and, in 1928, decided to leave the Soviet Union. My father left the USSR, disillusioned. They always talk about the white migration, but my father formed part of the laborers' migration, which left the Russian Revolution in order not to see the deep changes that were being talked about. He arrived in Argentina in 1929, and in 1930 I was born, the only Argentinian of the family.[11]

Once they arrived in Argentina, Joseph Gelman, his wife Paulina Burichson, and two children, Boris and Teodora, installed themselves in the city of Buenos Aires. In the beginning, his father worked in the Argentinian railroads; later he worked in carpentry and finally established himself as a merchant.

The life of Joseph Gelman was like the lives of many Ukrainian immigrants in Argentina during the beginning of the twentieth century. At the beginning, he was forced to go from job to job and support his family the best way he could. With time, he learned the Spanish of the River Plate region and could better manage his new home and the novel circumstances he had to face.

He didn't forget his distant Ukraine, his native language, or his political commitment. He accepted his destiny and believed that he left his family a promising future. Joseph Gelman died in 1964, on a cold autumn morning in his adopted city. Juan Gelman wrote the poem "El extranjero" ("The Foreigner"), which he published in *Cólera buey* (*Oxen Rage*), in honor of his father:

> With the cigar lit, my father used to walk hours and hours
> by the darkness of the dining room between the plants in
> the patio
> his wife used to say, "stop going around and around José"
> but he wouldn't want to eat nor sleep nor stop
> his feet wore away an afternoon
> he turned around and he closed his eyes like a birdy.[12]

In an interview by Rodolfo Braceli that appeared in *La Nación* in 2014, Gelman suggested that with the years, the figure of his father appeared in his memory with greater intensity. Eighty years old at that time, Gelman remembered his father more strongly and with a greater sense of his presence.

> —When you're around 80, is the presence of your parents felt?
> —Yes, it's intriguing, because I've felt the presence of my mother and lately I'm feeling the presence of my father. I see him through the poems I write. There were one, two, or even more affectionate gestures of remembrance. One time I was sick when I was 12 and he sat on the side of my bed and read tales of Sholem Aleichem in Yiddish. I remember that, but he was a silent man; for me, distant. And yet when he died in 1964, it took a lot to admit it, a lot. I came home, and they put the lid on the coffin, and I demanded that they lift it because I could not believe he had died. I was 34 and he was 74. Well, things in life happen. . . . Yes, in recent years my father has appeared. I do not know why it occurs because already. . . my kids, well, one was killed by the dictatorship; the other lives here and is over 50; for years, I have not lived with children. Maybe that's the reason why. I do not know.
> —Any other image of your dad?
> —Few words . . . then I began to understand his past. Within families they would talk little about important things. What happened during the immigration was left behind; draw the curtain and move on.[13]

His Mother and Grandfather, the Rabbi

Paulina Burichson, the daughter of Ukrainian rabbis from a family of humble origins, studied medicine in Odessa while finding time to indulge her passion for opera. Born in Balta, southwestern Ukraine, in 1897, she became the second wife of Joseph Gelman. In the following excerpt, Juan Gelman illustrates his mother's philosophy of life:

> Because of her rabbinic heritage, my mother had a way of understanding life where poverty exists. Yes, it is a fact, but human spirit does not end there. . . . For her love of music, she made us study piano.[14]

Paulina's father, Juan Gelman's maternal grandfather, was a marriage officer in a small *shtetl* (village) in Ukraine. The memory of Juan Gelman's grandfather will reach Juan filtered through the eyes of his mother, who described him as a sort of saint who ate only bread and tea. As Gelman says in the following passage, this reference will have significance in other traditions as well:

> Many years later in American poetry of the 1920s, I found reference to tea and bread in the words of many Jewish poets.[15]

Over time, Gelman understood the vital importance of his rabbi grandfather's memory for the whole family:

> I remember that the portrait of my grandfather, whom I never met, hung on the wall of my parents' bedroom: bearded, still in a turn-of-the-century photo with eyes that looked beyond what is seen. I know it scared me, but I do not know how. My mother would say that her father was better looking than I was, and that the one who looked like him was my son. The mysteries of inheritance . . . [16]

Paulina, like her son Juan, had also suffered the tragedy of a sibling's early death. According to Gelman, the Cossacks invaded her neighborhood one night and set fire to the home of little Paulina. Despite the desperate attempts of Paulina's mother, who entered the burning house to save her children, one of them lost her life in the fire:

> My childhood is full of extraordinary and terrible events that my mother told me about, like the day when the Cossacks, during a *pogrom*, burned everything, and my grandmother went into the burning house to save her children. She lost one. Every time there was danger, my grandfather pulled a small *arquilla* [small chest] with a parchment from approximately 1,700 CE and, paraphrasing Genesis, read, "this Rabbi begat this Rabbi, who begat this other Rabbi . . ." He was the last of the list. When there was a threat, reading the parchment gave them a sense of continuity and survival.[17]

The relationship between Juan Gelman and his mother transitioned through confusing, difficult, and intense periods. Over the years, Gelman reworked their complex coexistence much more clearly. Based on distant memories, letters, and old photographs, he remembered her as poor and persecuted, but also young, long-haired, beautiful, and idealistic:

> Odessa, 1915, you are 18 years old, you study medicine, there's nothing to eat / but your cheeks were rosy like apples (that's how you told it) (hunger tree that gives fruit) / had those apples the rosy color of the fire that burned your house? / at 5 years old? / Did your mother take from the burning house several siblings? / and your dead sister?[18]

Goodbye, Paulina

In 1982, when Gelman found exile in Nicaragua, he learned that his mother had died at eighty-five, after undergoing three operations for cancer. The poet received, all in one day, three letters referring to his mother that had been written at different times. He read first the one sent from the mother-in-law of his daughter, where she had seen his mother in a nursing home, found her active, planning conferences, and organizing the library.

The second was sent by his sister Teodora, who informed him that his mother had died. Finally, Gelman opened the third letter, sent by his own mother and dated twenty days earlier, in which she recalled distant memories and bid him farewell with a foreboding, "I am going to end this letter because I'm tired. . . ."[19]

From this bitter event arose the idea of writing *Carta a mi madre* (*Letter to My Mother*), his twenty-second book of poems, which begins:

> . . . I received your letter 20 days after your death, five minutes after knowing you were dead / a letter, you said, interrupted by your tiredness / they had seen you better then / sharp as ever / active at 85 years of age despite three operations for cancer that finally took you.[20]

The creative process for this new poetry collection spanned a period of seven years. From the time he learned of the death of his mother in 1982 until the time he finally published the work in Buenos Aires in 1989, the book was written in two distinct periods. The first version of the text was begun in Geneva and Paris; Gelman then abandoned this version to a drawer and forgot about it. Three years later, he opened the drawer and found it. He then proceeded to rewrite, clip, and complete the collection in the French capital during November 1987.

This new production, which Gelman dedicated to his sister, was presented in the form of a long monologue divided into twenty blocks. It demonstrated an existentially fragile Gelman facing the event of his mother's death. Her physical disappearance served as an existential trigger: Gelman wondered about the meaning of life as well as the nature of death and nothingness. Perhaps for this reason, the text abounds in questions and biographical references. His birth, for example, he remembered as if it were a first exile:

> I must have been very happy inside you / I would have loved to never have left from inside you / you drove me out and I expelled you.[21]

This farewell letter, taking the form of a visceral, direct, and radically honest soliloquy, presented two distinct stages. In the first, it is possible to read great existential uncertainty, with questions about all Gelman's issues of concern, from his relationship with his mother to the value and meaning of his poetry and his work. The literary voyage, full of memories and qualms, reveals a complex relationship with his mother, accurately setting forth the distance between them while seeking to meet her along the way:

> we rarely wrote to each other in these years of exile / it is also true that before we rarely spoke to each other / from very young, the one created for you rebelled against you / against your strict love / anger and sadness grew in me / you never laid a hand to hit me / you hit me with your soul.[22]

In the second stage, attempts at conciliation begin to appear. There is fullness and harmony, as though Gelman is testing an emergency landing after the hectic flight that began with the news of his mother's death. The journey, through turbulent and angry moments, slowly wings down until it culminates in Gelman's acceptance of his exile's reality, his love for his mother, and his poetic career's ultimate meaning.

Thus, the text also reserves a place for recognition, where neither distance nor loneliness can make him forget the tenderness of and communion with his mother:

> Give me the rage of your bones and I cradle them / you cradled me and I cradle your bones / who could distress the exile?[23]

Carta a mi madre is a confident exercise in conviction, reconciliation, and unconditional love, where initially everything falls apart. It then arms itself with new and old reasons that justify the effort.

Literature, a Family Legacy

Gelman discovered literature at an early age. At three years, he began to read and write. The fascination with books was part of a family legacy that his father began and his brother, Boris, continued. Boris was the son of Joseph Gelman's first wife and was twenty years older than Juan. It was Boris who would, early on, recite Pushkin's poems to Juan in Russian. Juan, only five years old, did not understand the meaning of the words, but he could get excited by their musicality and hypnotic rhythm.

Over the years, Gelman came to understand that it was those first readings that defined his later love of poetry:

> At that time, I discovered orally recited poetry. . . and started reading all my brother's books. He had a lot of those editions of Thor that I liked so much. These books were, at most, I think, 196 pages long. And no matter the progression of the story, when the novel got to that number of pages, it would stop right there.[24]

Later he would be seduced by the writings of Leo Tolstoy, Leonid Andreyev, and Victor Hugo, and by the literature of the Spanish Golden Age: Lope de Vega, Luis de Góngora, Garcilaso de la Vega, and Francisco de Quevedo:

> We were never locked in a ghetto, culturally or otherwise. Those years of my life coincided with World War II. For example, I did my *bar mitzvah*, because doing so filled life with meaning, amid the slaughter of Jews in Europe. But I received no religious education. What I remember most is that when I was thirteen I was given the complete works of Sholem Aleichem. My parents, who did not have a lot of money, saved pennies and once a year they would take us to the Opera House. There I heard frontline singers, splendid opera casts.[25]

He would then discover *Humiliated and Insulted* by Fyodor Dostoyevsky. With it, as mentioned in several interviews, came an unleashed passion for literature:

> I read it at age twelve and fell ill two days with fever. In my house, there was a metal ladder in the courtyard that reached the room where my brother slept. One Sunday I went to his room, took the book, and I devoured it from cover to cover.[26]

From an early age, Gelman lived in a multilingual environment: his brother read to him in Russian; his friends spoke Argentinian Spanish; at home, Ukrainian was spoken; and as a Jew, he would speak Yiddish, also a familiar language:

> In the 1930s, close to home there was a theater where they performed works in Yiddish. I think Kafka is right in what he discovered about the Yiddish theater; there must be something there that has to do with one's own family: for me this was the pain of the death of my mother's sister in a ghetto in Ukraine, and all those things that are transmitted familiarly.[27]

Ana's Knees and His First Poems

In addition to piano, English, French, and Latin lessons, as a nine-year-old child, Gelman played soccer with his classmates and began to develop a lifelong love of chess. But his concerns went beyond recreational and educational activities.

In mid-1939, he fell in love with Ana, an eleven-year-old neighbor to whom he had not been paying attention until then: "I loved her dirty knees. Verses of love came out of me, rhymes." The budding poet, to whom the neighbor did not seem to pay too much attention, tried reciting Almafuerte's[28] poems:

> Seduction yielded no results, so I thought I would have to write my own poems. I quickly started counting syllables with my fingers, as Marechal[29] would say. Anyway, I could never make her fall in love with me. From that disappointment, and from being a fan of the Atlanta soccer team, I was sad for a lifetime.[30]

In a text that appeared in *La Maga* magazine, in the issue dedicated to Gelman in 1997, Gelman adds:

> I'm not sure what was the first poem I wrote, but I know what was the first piece I published. We lived on the corner of Canning Avenue and Vera Street, and I was eight or maybe

> nine before I read a lot of poetry. Poetry was like hypnosis; I was attracted to the sounds on the one hand, and on the other the mystery of some incomprehensible words. . . .[31]

At eleven years, Gelman published his first poem in a literary magazine named *Rojo y Negro* (*The Red and the Black*).

State Terrorism. Family Portrait II

As a graduate of the National School of Buenos Aires, Gelman began to attend alumni meetings. There he met the woman who would be his first wife, Berta Shubaroff. An interview published in issue number three of the newspaper *Abuelas de Plaza de Mayo* in 2004 provides further details of the meeting:

> A friend of Berta had a group of friends from the National School of Buenos Aires alumni, with whom they began going out. Among them was Juan Gelman. Berta and Juan were the only ones who were not a couple, so they slowly began to become friends. One day, Berta confessed to Juan that she liked him, but Juan did not know what to say.

Months later, however, they became engaged, and they were married the following year.

In January 11, 1956, their eldest son, Marcelo Ariel Gelman Shubaroff, was born; the following year, his daughter, Nora Eva, made her appearance. According to the same interview, Marcelo's mother believed that Marcelo physically resembled his father. From her point of view, he had inherited "the meaning of love. He was very loving, affectionate, and had a great sense of humor."

The pleasant family events were quickly incorporated into the poet's early poems. In 1959, Gelman published his second book, *El juego en que andamos* (*The Game Which We Are In*), through the Nueva Expresión publishing company in Buenos Aires. In the section of that book entitled "Golpear el agua" ("Hitting the Water"), the poem titled "La hija" ("Daughter") refers to the newborn Nora Eva:

> She is as cheerful as the light that turns to see her / she talks a lot with the air / rises like summer. // Dances in solitude to make it a memory. / Tests that the world sings, / builds my innocence.[32]

The second section of the book, which has the same title as the book, "El juego en que andamos," consists of eight poems and reflects on the growth in infancy of his son Marcelo Ariel:

> He says the word poetry for the first time . . . Asks what is water. . . Smiles . . . I say how I love him.[33]

According to Gelman, his son showed an early political commitment:

> Marcelo had political concerns from childhood. At nine years old he surprised me with troubling questions, relevant ones, on Che and his slogan of creating several Vietnams in Latin America. I know from Marcelo's classmates that in elementary school he had already engaged in protest. Injustice bothered him. Bother is a very mild word for what he felt: anger. I also know that at age 14 he was in the Juventud Peronista (Peronist Youth) resistance movement, "putting the heat" to transnational companies. Like thousands of young people, he trusted Perón. He was 16, 17 years old and was deeply disappointed when Perón returned to government and supported the fascist Triple A. For those young militants that had fought for Perón's return and were later labeled "jóvenes imberbes" (beardless youths), disappointment did not confine them to passivity. He left the Juventud Peronista for the left, with the people from the Sabino Navarro Group. Disappointed again, he prowled the Ejército Revolucionario del Pueblo, ERP (People's Revolutionary Army), which also did not convince him. When they kidnapped him, he had no political affiliation, but he did have enough

> political history that the dictatorship considered him an enemy. They found his address in a book entry from an ERP girl. I am proud of my son's militancy. Sometimes I think I had something to do with it, and that redoubles my pride and my pain.

Marcelo, like his father, studied at the National School of Buenos Aires. During his time in high school, he experienced some of the same dislikes his father had experienced twenty years earlier: "Marcelo was a worried and sensitive young man," noted his mother in an interview published in the newspaper *Abuelas de Plaza de Mayo* in 2004. "He wanted to leave the school to meet boys from different social classes, kids outside the aristocratic class who went to the School of Buenos Aires; then he enrolled in the Manuel Belgrano School."

The Kidnapping of His Children: *"I Do Not Want Other News but You"*

On August 24, 1976, five months after the coup d'état that overthrew the weak government of María Estela Martínez de Perón, paramilitaries kidnapped Nora Eva, age nineteen; Marcelo Ariel, age twenty; and his wife, María Claudia Irureta Goyena, age nineteen, who was seven months pregnant. When Nora Eva was kidnapped by Argentinians and Uruguayans, they forced her to lead them to the home of Marcelo. After they found the home, they took Nora, Marcelo Ariel, and his wife as detainees.

Forty-eight hours after the event, Nora Eva was released. Marcelo Ariel and María Claudia would never again be seen alive.

According to Ana Laura Pérez in an article that appeared in *Clarín*, the sad denouement of Marcelo Ariel occurred within two months of his kidnapping. Thirteen years later, in 1989, following an investigation conducted by the Argentine Forensic Anthropology Team, Gelman learned that his son, kidnapped and imprisoned in the concentration camp Automotores Orletti, had been executed. He was shot in the neck from two feet away on the night of October 21, 1976. He was placed in a barrel, which was then filled with a mixture of sand and cement and thrown into the Luján River. Juan Gelman recovered the remains of his son on October 14, 1989.

Letter to Marcelo Ariel: *"Where Are You/ Lukewarm Sad?"*

Carta abierta (*Open Letter*), the thirteenth book of poems by Gelman, consists of twenty poems dedicated to the memory of Marcelo Ariel, as is clearly stated in the epigraph: "To my son."

Despite the personally tragic subject matter of the poems, its title, *Carta abierta*, shows it to be a text attempting to reach as many readers as possible: Gelman felt an obligation to tell the world about the consequences of state terrorism in Argentina.

The title refers to two texts that denounce blows to the rule of law: "Carta abierta a la Junta Militar" ("Open Letter to the Military Junta"), written by Rodolfo Walsh, and *Catilinarias* by Marco Tulio Cicerón. The correspondences between the three texts demonstrate the testimonial character of these letters, which have acquired the status of historical documents.

Carta abierta does not directly address military officers of the Junta Militar, to which Gelman elusively alludes through images like "*perros de la contra*" (dogs of the opposition) or "*muros de la muerte*" (walls of death). As do the other two texts, it speaks of the terrible consequences of the coup, mainly focusing on the disappearance, torture, and murder of his son Marcelo Ariel and many other *compañeros*.

The anguish that Gelman poured into the text takes on different forms. Gelman relies upon a novel deployment of resources. First, we see a meticulous lexical deconstruction, with the invention of words like *soledadera*, *carnemente*, *sufridera*, and *desquerés* (solitudiness, meatly, sufferive, and nowant). He also converted nouns into verbs, transformed masculine nouns into feminine, and adopted the unexpected use of diminutives. The idea seems to be to show the difficulties encountered when seeking means to express and describe the indescribable: horror and personal tragedy.

Second, a constant use of the prefix "des" (un) populates this open letter:

> "talking to you or untalking to you/ my pain/"
> "having you/ unhaving you/"
> "my heart/ unhearting of me/"
> "tying?/ untying?/")

The "des" (un) particle puts the absence of the beloved on display. The thematic unit is absence; absence not only of the missing child, but also of the distant homeland. Thus, Gelman became both a territorial exile and an exile from paternity. He is a father *despadrado* (unfathered); a father that has been *deshijado* (unsonned.). In VII the poet says: *"deshijándote mucho/deshijándome"* (unsonning you a lot/ unsonning me).

This strategy proposes a set of symmetries that the poet addresses with antonyms "do/ undo," "wait/ unwait," and "die/ undie." Forming these antonyms with the prefix *des* (un) produces an effect combining opposition with repetition. In the sequence *do/ undo*, the sound *do* is pronounced twice. This repetition is linked to the theme of memory: Repeat, to not forget. Repetition reinforces the memory of the absent, as though we were at a political rally, repeating the slogan with the logic of hammering.

Third, we note the appearance of many verses that organize their rhythm around the consonant *m*, as if the sound is meant to invoke the *m*emory and name of his son, Marcelo Ariel.

> *. . . voluntad que no mira tu mirada/ memoria que amarísima*
> *de muere/ amarillea al pie de tu otoñar/ memoria que morís*
> *con*
> *¿como otro mundo?/ humildemente amando?/*
> *. . . ¿me sentás a la mesa de tu alma?/*
>
> (. . . will that does not look at your look/ memory that so in
> love of dies/ yellowed at the foot of your autumn/ memory that
> dies with
> like another world?/ humbly loving?/
> . . . do you sit me at the table of your soul? /)

The conspicuous absence of capital letters in proper names and at the beginning of sentences in this collection constitutes the fourth strategy, which tries to convey a greater sense of dispossession. The absence of the loved one seems to correspond to the lack of capitalization. It is likely that the strategy of not observing the rules of capitalization minimizes the importance of a particular person in order to focus on all other individuals. Such is the case in the "tens of thousands of other cases," not named, that were deprived of their rights as human beings, like Marcelo Ariel.

XVII

I do not want other news but of you/
any other is a little breadcrumb where
memory dies of starvation/ digging up
to continue looking for you/ it becomes
crazy with darkness/ fired its bitch/
burns apart/ watch your look
absent/ mirror where I do not see myself/
you turn off this shadow with mercury/ you crackle/
I cold sweat when I believe I hear/
you/ cold of love I lie in my half
of you/ I do not finish finishing/
it is clear I understand that I do not understand

On Thursday March 31, 2011, after a long process, the Oral Federal Court No. 1 sentenced the repressors of the clandestine center Automotores Orletti. By doing so, the court condemned the military responsible for the kidnapping, torture, and murder of Marcelo Ariel Gelman, among other victims of the military dictatorship.

Political Convictions

Juan Gelman's interest in political militancy as a tool for social change came from his past. His father, Joseph Gelman, who described himself as a man of revolutionary convictions, was an anti-monarchical fighter, an exile, and a victim of the police harassment of Czar Nicholas II.

The life of his father greatly influenced Juan. It functioned as a kind of mold with which he fashioned part of his biography. In fact, his and his father's lives had a great deal in common. The two shared hopes and miseries, political commitment, persecution, exile, and ultimately, family tragedy.

Four well-defined moments may be identified in the political life of Juan Gelman.

Gelman started his political comittment at age fifteen, when he joined the Communist Party of Argentina.

The death of Che Guevara in 1967 precisely marks the beginning of the second part of his journey. The effect this news had on Gelman, like it had on many other young Argentinians, was to cause him to join the Fuerzas Armadas Revolucionarias (FAR) (Revolutionary Armed Forces). This Marxist-Leninist organization decided to follow the path of armed struggle, inspired by the theories of Guevara.

With the confluence of FAR and Montoneros that took place on October 12, 1973, Gelman began his third and final militant period. In this case, he followed the leadership of the Montoneros.

The fourth and final stage of Gelman's political journey coincided with his break with the Montoneros in 1979. Already separated from all political party structure, Gelman began the long task of self-criticism and initiated a period of political protest and social activism independent of any political party apparatus.

Stage 1 (1936–1964) The Communist Party

From childhood, Gelman showed clear signs of interest in political and social issues. It is no wonder; the historical period in which he lived was full of significant political events and transcendent warfare: the Spanish Civil War; the confrontation between Peronists and anti-Peronists, which marked political Argentinian life for decades; and finally, World War II, which divided the world into two sides and opened the equally bloody Cold War period, which would include the wars in Korea, Vietnam, and Afghanistan.

The outbreak of the Spanish Civil War particularly mobilized Gelman. In more than one text he has recalled how his father Joseph would send him every night to buy the journal *Crítica*, which sympathized with the Republicans, so that he could monitor the progress of the fighting. In 1936, at six years old, Juan participated in his first militant action in support of the Republicans: "With the other kids in the neighborhood, we collected chocolate tinfoils because we believed that these would be bullets for the anti-Franco Regime."[34] The local climate was rife with debate and confrontation, as if the Spanish conflict had moved to the Buenos Aires streets. Francoists and Republicans took part in discussions that were so passionate they seemed endless. Gelman, like many others of his generation, felt like a son of the Spanish democratic cause.

This, joined to the increasing division between Peronists and anti-Peronists, provided a basis for his active political participation.

> And later came World War II. I began high school, and in the neighborhood and at school most people favored the allies. . . . All these factors, summed up in the rising of Peronism and anti-Peronism, permeated the life of much of the population and pushed for the political participation of many young people. I was one of them.[35]

Gelman completed his high school studies between 1943 and 1947. As a son of an immigrant worker, he had to survive the new experience of coexisting with classmates with a more distinctive social standing than his. Most students were children of the military, the oligarchy, and the proprietor class. But the coexistence was peaceful. Without being an extraordinary student, he divided his days between the rigor demanded by his studies and more enjoyable popular pursuits. He managed this by alternating student activities with billiards at Cafe San Bernardo, the game of dice, dominoes, and the *milonga*:[36]

> The military and oligarchy's children studied in the National School of Buenos Aires. I wasn't either of the two, and besides, I was Jewish. But they never messed with me much. After class, I returned to the neighborhood, to Villa Crespo, to "the boys" who didn't go to the National School. With these fifteen- and sixteen-year-olds, I got to know the downtown area.[37]

Gelman's interest in the causes that he considered fair brought him closer to political militancy. At age fifteen, he entered the Communist Youth:

> My dad didn't like it too much that I militated in the Communist Party, because he had already been "burned," as he said. Many hopes had been placed in the Russian Revolution. And ten years later, he had to confront an enormous disappointment. Because of this he always distrusted left-wing militancy. On the other hand, what preoccupied my mom was the fact that I returned very late and had not yet eaten dinner. I guess it is a typical mother's reproach, right?[38]

These were also the years in which the Labor Party rose and Juan Perón quickly ascended into national politics.

> It was Perón's time, and the bar divided in two: They were the Peronists and we were the "democrats." It was interesting, for momentarily we came not to talk to each other. Fifteen years old and we already had ideological rivals! But I didn't hate the Peronists. In reality, I never broke it off with these men or they with me. We were united by common histories: girlfriends,

> *milongas*, bar hours. . . . I remember . . . the coup d'état of 1943, the advent of Peronism and the coup d'état of 1955. That is to say there had been an atmosphere, a context of huge social effervescence in all these years that, without a doubt, permeated our attitude as practitioners.[39]

The spontaneous and popular mobilization of 1945 that gave birth to the Peronist movement would also remain in his political conscience. The unexpected and ragtag collection of workers and skilled workforce—in the words of writer Raúl Scalabrini Ortiz, "*el subsuelo de la patria sublevado*" (the rebellious subsoil of the fatherland)— arose from the industrial suburbs of Buenos Aires to demand the release of Perón.

> Parading before my eyes swarthy faces, brawny arms, beefy torsos, with matted hair in the air and scant garments covered with the remains of tars, oils, and fats. They came singing and shouting, begging for one name: Perón. It was the most heterogeneous crowd that imagination can conceive. The traces of their origins were reflected on their countenances. The descendant of southern Europeans walked with the blond of Nordic traits, and the olive-skinned native of stiff hair in which the blood of a distant Indian yet survived. . . . That crowd advanced in this way, into threads of enthusiasms that arrived along Avenida de Mayo, by Balcarce, the Diagonal. . . . They came from the plants of Puerto Nuevo, from the workshops of Chacarita and Villa Crespo, from the factories of San Martín and Vicente Lopez, from the foundries and steel mills of the Riachuelo, from the spinning mills of Barracas. They broke out from the swamps of Gerli and Avellaneda, or down from the Lomas de Zamora. United in the same cry and the same faith walk together the farm worker of Cañuelas and the precision turner, the foundry mechanical worker of automobiles, the spinner, and the laborer. They were the rebellious subsoil of the fatherland.[40]

In 1964, seduced by the mysticism of the Peronist Movement and disenchanted by the practices of the Argentinian Communist Party, "absolutely convinced of the party's belonging to the right wing," as

Gelman would say in an interview appearing in *La Maga*, he definitively moved away. The rupture included the separation of the literary group, *El Pan Duro* (Stale Bread), founded by Gelman and closely linked to the Communist Party.

> Something odd: They threw me out of the PC[41] for quitting. It's a serious case! There was a discussion: I was the correspondent of the Chinese agency in the country and the leadership of the PC wanted me to quit. I didn't understand: for me, China was still a revolution, although they were not allied with the Soviet Union. I didn't discuss the international issue, I discussed the national political ways. And a moment arrived in which there was no room for discussion. So I wrote to the Chinese, saying that if they wanted me out of the agency, I would gladly leave. They replied to me that there was no way, that they wanted me to stay. I left the party in May of 1964. One month later, the general secretary decided to expel me. It seems that this is the custom of all the communist parties. Once, in Paris, the mayor of a small town invited me to eat alongside a poet from the French PC. This poet wanted me to tell the mayor the truth about my expulsion. I told him, and the mayor, impudent, said, "Naturally, it's normal."[42]

The first books written by Gelman are populated with figures and references to revolutionary poets and heroes from the Communist Party. We will reflect upon this emerging political conviction as it is found in the following four books: *Violín y otras cuestiones* (*Violin and Other Issues*), *El juego en que andamos*, *Gotán* (*Tango*), and *Cólera buey.*

In his first book of 1956, *Violín y otras cuestiones,* containing a prologue by Raúl González Tuñón, Gelman launched a litany of rebellious images against what he believed to be unjust. In the second part of the book, titled "Viendo a la gente andar" ("Watching People Walk Along"), there are two poems that are significant because of their originality and political harshness: "Oración de un desocupado" ("Prayer of the Unemployed") and "Niños: Corea 1952" ("Children: Korea 1952"). The first, with clear tones of heresy and protest, proposes the hard image of a careless, neglectful, and apparently indifferent God.

Father,
. . . Come down from the skies, if you are here, come
down then,
that I die of hunger in this corner,
that I don't know of what purpose my birth serves,
that I see my hands rejected,
that there is no work, there is none
come down a little, contemplate,
this that I am, this broken shoe,
this anguish, this empty stomach,
this city without bread for my teeth, the fever
digging into my flesh,
this way of sleep,
under the rain, punished by the cold, persecuted,
I tell you I don't understand, Father, come down . . . [43]

The second poem of this section, "Niños: Corea 1952," which displays a lyrical-political irreverence and compromise, including scenes from the war contesting the two Koreas, supported by the United States and the People's Republic of China, are used as poetic material.

Little brothers . . . How it hurts
to learn to count by bombers
with the sky as blackboards!
How it hurts, little brothers,
to know by heart the "h" of hunger
and to know the death by heart
and to know the Yankees of pure hatred,
how it hurts, little brothers! . . .

(Do not sleep, boy.
Do not sleep darling.
Because in the rice fields
the invader is killing.
Do not sleep boy.
Not yet . . .)[44]

These first poems reflect this double capacity that González Tuñón highlighted in his prologue. The author of *La calle del agujero en la media* (*The Hole in the Sock Street*) underlined Gelman's capacity to speak of social themes ("he's not an escapee from reality"), without eluding "the luxury of fantasy" and "rich and sharp lyricism." On this point, there is an increasing consensus in specialized literary criticism: Gelman is not "an editorialist in verse," Tuñón says, but a versatile writer who can address issues of a "social nature" without abandoning an aesthetic and exquisite criterion.

In 1959, Gelman published his second book of poems, *El juego en que andamos*. In one of the compositions, he alludes to the life and will of Pepe Díaz, a Nicaraguan soldier who fights and falls alongside Augusto César Sandino in 1934. The death of soldier Díaz implies not only a defeat, but also a life lesson for his son, which he will transform forty-five years later, in the Sandinista victory of 1979.

Will of Pepe Díaz, Soldier[45]
Nicaragua, 1934

By the marsh, the defeated air,
the birds, hats, boots, fears,
the death walks, rides a horse, this is over,
cheers for what we were, or better
cheers for what we will be,

cups pass by

toasting for the shot that awaits you,
beware of dying,
of not dropping a card, a glove,
a single kiss from a woman, the moon,
the hungers you have passed, the hole
where you went to urinate, the sweet bed
of making a son by hits of love,
of not dying like this,

the general

Sandino is looking at the ground.
All of his blood looks to the ground.

And there we will walk, pepe, leaning back.
Our children will tell that we were parents
to deserve them, they will rise burning
what we are, gunpowder or ash,
they'll have their Nicaragua spring,
liberty, peace, tablecloth, coffee, violets.

And then we will live like I tell you.
There, in the future.

Because today it is time to die as men.

The first section of *Gotán*, Gelman's fourth book, published in 1962, included two poems in which social preoccupations are a recurrent literary motif: "María la sirvienta" ("María the Maid") and "Pedro el albañíl" ("Pedro the Bricklayer"), which recounts the story of a Republican Spanish immigrant who dies on the scaffolding with "*su cuchara llena de rabia*" (his spoon full of rage), remembering his murdered companions during the Spanish Civil War.

"María la sirvienta" crudely exposes the hypocrisy of Argentina's middle and upper classes in the mid-twentieth century regarding the feared and hidden issue of abortion and infanticide.

She was called María for all her 17 years,
she was able to have soul and smile with birdies,
but the important thing was that they found in her suitcase
a three days old dead child who had been wrapped in
newspapers from the house.

What way to sin to sin was that,
said the women used to the secrecy
and in the signal of horror they raised their eyebrows
with a brief flight, not devoid of charm.

The men quickly reflected on the dangers

of the prostitution or of the lack of prostitution,
reminisced their exploits with various harlots
and said harshly: ofcoursedear.

At the police station, they were decent with her,
the sergeant and higher-ranking officer were the only
ones who touched her,
but María spent her time crying,
the birdies smudged beneath the rain of tears.[46]

In an interview that Gelman had with Mexican Subcomandante Marcos, writer and ex-deputy commander of the Zapatista Army of the National Liberation, Marcos recounted the impact that the reading of this poem had upon him.

—Do you still read poetry?

—Yes, of course. In some of the reports I tell the story of a girl that dies, Paticha, explaining a little of the unborn theme. In reality, that came from the reading of a poem by an Argentinian that speaks of a little girl. Do you recall this poem? What's it called?

—I don't know the poem that you're talking about.

—It's yours.

—There are things that one wants to forget, I tell you.

—No, the poem is good. I found it in an anthology of Latin American poetry, along with another text of yours. I don't remember what it is called, but it talks about a girl who, obligated by social conditions, commits a crime.

—Was it "María the Maid?"

—Ahh, that's it. Your structure inspired the literary form of the story of Paticha. The story is real, but its presentation is very close to "María the Maid."

Contrasts exist between the indigenous child, Paticha, who dies of fever at age five, and "María la sirvienta." "En unas horas, una calentura le quemó los años y los sueños" (In a few hours, a temperature burned her years and her dreams), wrote Subcomandante Marcos of Paticha in a text appearing in Mexico in 2001.

The second part of *Gotán,* titled "Como esperanza" ("As Hope"), returns to the idea of a sudden social change. The revolutionary theme appears as an indication of Gelman's obsession: "se fue otro mes / y no hicimos la revolución todavía" (another month passed / and we still didn't make the revolution). This is evident in the nine poems that compose the section. In this context, the collection includes a poem titled, "La vez que vi a Jiří Wolker" ("The Time I Saw Jiří Wolker"), in tribute to young poet Wolker, who founded the Czech Communist Party in 1921 and died of tuberculosis at age twenty-four. The third section, titled "Cuba sí," is composed of six poems that celebrate the Cuban revolution and culture: "Habana Revisited," "Fidel," "Camilo Cienfuegos," and "Carta a Roberto Fernández Retamar, Habana" ("Letter to Roberto Fernández Retamar, Havana").

The case of *Cólera buey,* his fifth book, is quite interesting because two different versions appeared: The first was edited in La Habana in 1965, and the extended version was published in Buenos Aires in 1971. The volume of La Habana comprised poems written between 1962 and 1965. Much of the first version continues to appeal to Communist Party symbolism, with references to many of its militants and heroes. Therefore, it may well be considered part of his first militant stage.

However, the more complete version includes a long poem dedicated to the figure of Che Guevara. It incorporates sarcastic comments about the Argentinian Communist Party and its bureaucratic structures. For this reason, we have excluded this new version from his first political stage and have placed it in the second, which Gelman ascribes to the strategies of the Fuerzas Armada Revolucionarias.

References to political matters stand out among the main issues of the first version of *Cólera buey.* Attending to these ideas, one can find in this collection of poems references to village struggles that occurred in the

Democratic Republic of the Congo, Vietnam, and Algeria. It mentions Patrice Émery Lumumba—anti-colonial leader of the former Belgian Congo, now the Democratic Republic of the Congo; Jiří Wolker, mentioned previously in *Gotán;* and Hungarian poet Attila Jószef, who, like Wolker, committed to the outlawed Communist Party and died at an early age.

> Jiří Wolker, Attila Jószef, and I
> would be three perfect friends.
> Jiří talked about Prague,
> about the blind stoker's eyes looking at us.
> Jószef sang to Flora and the Revolution
> and there were no trains for suicidal people
> nor hospital beds to die in.[47]

In this collection of poems, one can see that Gelman's intention was clear: international solidarity does not acknowledge customs or national attributions. To the same degree as Wolker and Jószef, Gelman shared a preference for words and lyrical expression: They were born in the beginning of the twentieth century, shared similar ideological visions of the world, and were all poets. The selection does not seem capricious. The need to redeem these poets and the nationalist fighters such as Lumumba shows that solidarity is international, like poetic sensitivity:

> this ended like we had always wanted
> in a barricade
> Jiří, Jószef and I finally whistling

Stage 2 (1967–1973) The Revolutionary Armed Forces (FAR)

The second phase of Gelman's political-ideological journey began with the cold-blooded assassination of Ernesto "Che" Guevara de la Serna, on October 7, 1967. After this brutal murder, Gelman decided to join the Revolutionary Armed Forces.

The Revolutionary Armed Forces emerged in 1966 as a guerrilla force led by Carlos Enrique Olmedo and Roberto Jorge Quieto. This group had a Guevarist and Marxist orientation and were reputed to have good operational technicians. It was believed that they had demolished Minimax supermarkets—property of the Rockefeller Group—and had taken over the city of Garín—one of the most remembered actions by a group of which Gelman was a part.

On July 30, 1970, approximately thirty militants of the FAR would take over the most important institutions of Garín within a four-hour time frame. During that time, they would immobilize personnel and take over the telephone station (to leave the city incommunicado), the provincial bank (where they stole a significant amount of money), the police station (to avoid police repression), and the main access road to the town (to stop possible reinforcement that could arrive from local neighbors). The operation was successful and marked the initiation of the organization.

The following day, the newspaper *Clarín* published an announcement from the Revolutionary Armed Forces; it stated that the guerrilla fighters had a note hidden behind the men's bathroom mirror in a bar in Caseros and Montes de Oca, Buenos Aires. In this message, they said they were members of the Revolutionary Armed Forces and explained the reasons for their struggle, which they described as triggered by the following historical events: the death of Che Guevara, the coup of 1955, the execution of General Juan José Valle, and the torture and assassinations of "the people's heroes and martyrs" (such as Felipe Vallese, Santiago Pampillón, Emilio Jáuregui, and Emilio Maza), and, finally, the fact that there was no longer a path to carry forward the political fight through democratic means ("the armed fight is imposed on us as the only way out"). They ended the announcement with a slogan: "Free or dead, we are never enslaved. Ever onward to victory! The Revolutionary Armed Forces."

The group's activities became less frequent as some of their members became imprisoned.

This second militant political phase of Gelman has its literary correlation, especially in three of his poetry collections: *Cólera buey* (the second version), *Fábulas* (*Fables*), and *Relaciones* (*Relations*).

With the death of Che, many young leftists around the world considered, as did Gelman, taking more assertive roles and initiating numerous radical actions. The impact of Che's death is reflected in the second version of *Cólera buey*.

The tenth section of this second version, titled "Pensamientos (Octubre de 1967)" ("Thoughts [October 1967]") is organized around a single verse that repeats ten times: "I am from a country where . . . " This line serves as a marker of national origin and as a starting point for a political, social, poetic, and socioeconomic analysis in a historical context of many contradictions. Repetition structures the poetic subject's thought, which progressively eliminates contradictions toward the end. In the list of culprits, including those who appear to be part of the Argentinian Communist Party, condemnation for Che Guevara's death appears to be irreversible.

> . . . you mummies of the Communist Party of Argentina
> you let him down
> you doubtful leftists
> you let him down
> you owners of the revealed truth
> you let him down . . .
> you that looked at China without knowing that
> in reality, looking at China
> was looking at our country
> you let him down
> you insignificant theoreticians,
> talking about taking action
> through post mail supporters
> through the phone,
> or through metaphysical manifestations
> you let him down
> you empty priests of the guerrilla warfare
> you let him down
> you members of the fat asses club
> seated on "the reality"
> you let him down . . .
>
> you who don't believe in magic
> you let him down

I am from a country where commander Guevara
was let down:
the military officers, the priests, the homeopaths
the public auctioneers,
the Jewish masochistic Spanish refugees
the bosses and
also the laborers for now[48]

The sequence continues, and those assigned responsibility seem inexcusable. At the end of the poem, the poet includes himself among those responsible for the death of Che:

. . . I am from a country where I myself
let him down

This type of progressive sincerity or evolutionary self-criticism shows the extent of his discouragement, where sadness and anger mix. The poem slowly begins to delimit this universe of frustrations, where disorientation and the need to promote an internal debate in the revolutionary organizations appear: Who is responsible for Che Guevara's death? From this question arise clearly implied interrogatives that the poem continues to mention. Different revolutionary leftist and militant organizations began at that time to think that the only option left was to fight with weapons; Gelman agreed with them. In the poem, this historical situation takes the form of a choral ensemble, whose gabbled discussions arise with accusations and affirmations, opening and closing with an emphasis on "You." The poem's repetition of "you let him down," which readers read and repeat many times, function like the "amen" that parishioners repeat at the end of a prayer. This device gives this elegiac poem an almost religious tone. The poem opens with a type of dialogue with the murdered, where the poet confesses his limits and inexperience:

I know few things / I know that I should not mourn,
Ernesto

When Che was in Bolivia, Juan Gelman's name appeared in his diary. The diary suggested that Gelman would have supported Che as leader of an armed group. In an interview done by Susana Viau, Gelman recalled the moment when he learned about the *Diario* and his appearance in it:

> —Did it surprise you when the radio announced that they had seized the *Diario del Che* and that Juan Gelman was mentioned in it as one of his men in Argentina?
>
> —I didn't know anything. That morning I was working on *Panorama* and Pajarito García Lupo called to tell me, "Juan, you are mentioned in a best-seller."

In the years following the death of Che Guevara, political violence began to increase in Argentina. The right-wing death squads, created by the minister of social welfare, José López Rega, began the cycle of kidnappings and assassinations with the support of federal and local authorities. The revolutionary Peronism, with its leader in exile and dead since 1974, along with Marxist groups (both followers in the Communist Party and in different Trotskyite organizations), and even the Catholic Church (as if it were part of a medieval ritual) all participated actively in the party of blood.

With the publication of *Fábulas* in 1971, his seventh book of poems, these issues, above all those related to the armed fight, would appear tightly themed. In "Siglas" ("Acronyms"), for example, Gelman portrayed the climate of tension of the period in an explicit way, including the idea that people could achieve justice by their own hands.

> oh mary of salvation
> they had already prayed enough
> when the sky fell on them
> when the dirt covered them
> and their eyes, mouths, or children
> get tired in the same
> painful darkness
> which devoured their kidneys
> and this didn't let them breathe

this didn't let them dream like
small human pieces that
would crackle like dogs
then, love-armed they lighted up
against the ink of their landlords

ah birds of passion
writing all over the wall
FAP, ERP, FAR or strong forces
that stood up one day
against the dirty the dishonor
the embarrassment that grew in our skin
without deserving it
in the mother that gave birth to us
in the son that we gave birth to
like an abrupt mirror or
an emancipated midpoint
they kept walking over the-country
and awakening the-value
still, the-dark dog

When prayers weren't enough to end the kids' fevers and diseases in the solitude of the night, Gelman would say, "When there's no bread or water to satisfy their thirst, anger and fury arise, outrage is loved and armed (*amadarma*) to confront the oppressor's machinery." With this clear objective, the poet explains, "strong forces" emerged and arose one day to combat the inequality of opportunities in the desolate nights. "*Siglas*" offers a panorama of the reality of Argentinian politics in the 1970s, from a poetic point of view, where guerrilla organizations like the FAP (Fuerzas Armadas Peronistas—Peronist Armed Forces), ERP, and FAR gradually went underground.

There are two very remarkable characteristics that are visible at the syntactic and morphological level of the poem that seem to bring forth issues related to institutional breakdown. The first involves the "regularization" of certain irregular verbs that are conjugated in a preschool way: *quisió*, *tuvió*, *seducíó* (wanted, had, seduced). His other strategy is to disrupt the gender of some nouns, transforming masculine nouns into feminine: *la mundo*, *una camino*, *una planeta*, *una calor* (the world, sadness, a road, a planet, heat). Here Gelman tries to feminize the masculine world of these "fables," where male figures are the majority. The purpose of these strategies is to cause the reader to stop, astonished and startled, and to reread and realize the implications of these new meanings.

With the publication of *Fábulas*, Gelman intended to build a transversal anthology composed of exemplary stories of social fighters, poets, and other countercultural figures. Stories in this new collection vary, and include, among others, the names of liberator José Gervasio Artigas (in "Ríos") ("Rivers"); writers Leopoldo Marechal (in "Caras") ("Faces") and Comte de Lautréamont (in "Sudamericanos") ("South Americans"); and a reporter, Emilio Jáuregui (in "Muerte de Emilio Jáuregui") ("Death of Emilio Jáuregui"). Jáuregui was assassinated by the repressive forces of Juan Carlos Onganía's de facto government when he was twenty-nine.

Among the Europeans mentioned in the series are Almirante Horatio Nelson ("Ojo") ("Eye"), Aimé Bonpland ("El botánico") ("The Botanist"), and, finally, Catalan anarchist Joaquín Penina. Penina was assassinated by José Felix Uriburu's government, the first de facto government in Argentinian history, and is mentioned in three of the sixteen poems that are part of the series: "Madres" ("Mothers"), "Fábula encontrada donde" ("Fable Found Where"), and "Consecuencias" ("Consequences").

The new book sought to find examples that were up to date with the drama of political events at the time. The series, which is quite heterodox, includes well-known people from different areas (Uruguay, France, Spain, and Argentina) and different ethnic-cultural backgrounds (indigenous people, Europeans, and Creoles). These fables allude to wild stories: There are collective suicides, people executed by dictatorships, different matricides, enamored admirals, and scientists attracted by the voluptuousness of America's land.

Gelman's eighth book of poems, *Relaciones* (*Relations*), written between 1971 and 1973, was released in 1973. The new book closely followed the strategies employed in *Fábulas* and coincides with Rafael Alberti's poetic approach, which was known as "the poet in the street." Alberti believed that an alert and attentive poet should be on the street, witnessing the new public manifestations.

In this piece of work, various types of stories come together. Eduardo Galeano states in the prologue to the 1980 Lumen edition that these are different "faces of the world." Among them appear the face of Toussaint Louverture, the Haitian liberator who died incarcerated ("Notas") ("Notes"); the faces of the six crazy nurses from Pickapoon Hospital who burned to death ("Preguntas") ("Questions"); the faces of exploited miners who extracted tungsten from the mines in San Luis, Argentina ("Escrituras") ("Writings"); the face of the indigenous Lobo Amarillo challenging the official history of the white man ("Defectos") ("Defects"); and the dirty face of the little beggar on the train ("Abrigos") ("Coats"). Also included are the faces of Federico García Lorca, shot in Granada ("Rojos") ("Reds"); of the Polish Jew, Lubchik Nachalnik, incarcerated in Auschwitz ("Comidas") ("Foods"); of the lumberjack, Ildefonso Godoy, who paradoxically died in poverty when working ("Noticias") ("News"); of the homeless woman in the main square ("Reuniones") ("Reunions"); of Walt Whitman ("Cautelas") ("Cautions"); and of the prisoner, Eugenio, suffering in Villa Devoto jail ("Cambios") ("Changes"), where he probably met his military *compañero* and poet, Francisco Urondo.[49] In prison Urondo wrote, "La verdad es la única realidad" ("Truth is the only reality"). In this poem he reflected on the "ineffectiveness" of prison bars, which deprived him of freedom but did not prevent or postpone his dream of revolution ("Reconocimiento") ("Recognition").

This list could continue with many other representatives of underprivileged groups, of the poor and subalterns, who "no pasan el día acariciados por jamaicanas de talles de palmera" (don't spend their days cherished by Jamaican girls the size of palm trees), as we read in "Situaciones" ("Situations").

> they don't spend their days surrounded by the green birds
> singing
> they don't spend their days cherished by Jamaican girls the size
> of palm trees
>
> . . . they are attacked by fury and sorrow
> the opposing power works on their faces, hearts and lungs
> poison fills their mouths that external injustice rushes from
> their interior
> they spit venom around sometimes
>
> . . . in the middle of the night they hear gunshots

they hear, in the middle of the night, gunshots
they hear gunshots in the middle of the night
in the middle of the night they hear[50]

These are not examples of successful people in society. They are the oppressed villagers who hear gunshots in the middle of the night. They are those who are immersed in a dark reality, far from the "green birds singing." They are the permanent guides to Gelman's poetry, which corresponds more in each iteration to a double (and more than double) biography: his own biography, but also the biography/history of his country; and, gradually adding a third and fourth dimension, the biography/history of the region and of the whole world. Uruguayan critic Ángel Rama thought that this portrayal originated from the poet's own conscience:

> This reality is the transformed action in which fit destructions, reworkings, and metamorphosis. Although these poems don't tell or sing actions, but rather are born from interstices, as occupations of brief pauses in which conscience assumes, refracts, and reflects on the sum of accumulated actions. There aren't more than 60 poems for a completed decade, which make the speech of an ardent conscience, hurt and critical, in such a way that they should be read on the brilliant and nameless background of a turbulent and tragic succession. . . like soliloquies of a conscience that argues, analyzes, recalls, or chants happiness.[51]

Stage 3 (1973–1979) Montoneros

Both organizations, the Revolutionary Armed Forces and the Montoneros, decided to merge on October 12, 1973. Their ideologies were not very different, and they shared several military strategies.

In 1973, with Gelman having recently been incorporated into the Montoneros, the organization faced an internal debate. There were several issues discussed concerning the pros and cons of being underground. Gelman believed that there was leeway to continue acting in legality, more like a political party. The Montoneros had several representatives in both chambers of the legislature, and had carried out an important project based in low-income neighborhoods. With the rise of violence started by the fascist Triple A, the Montoneros decided to respond with the same currency: "The answer was the same, and that wasn't the best answer . . . " said Gelman in an interview in 1997.

> In 1974, the organization decided to go underground, when there were really still ways they could have acted through political discussion. . . . By going underground, forgive me for the expression, the leadership left peoples' asses in the air. . . . It was political suicide; the base's structure did not have a means of escaping the persecution of Triple A. The people that worked in the shanty towns, at the refrigeration factories, only had one way to save themselves; they had to leave their home and job. But "where did the people go to find another job?"[52]

On March 24, 1976, the National Armed Forces perpetrated a coup d'état against the federal government and the rule of law. Gelman was already exiled in Rome for doing what the Montoneros required. A few months after the coup, the military forces assassinated his *compañero*, the poet Francisco "Paco" Urondo. "At that moment, Paco Urondo and I were the same age: 42 and 43 years old," Gelman recalled. Finding out about the death, he wrote "Carta a Paco Urondo" ("Letter to Paco Urondo") on May 29, 1980, while exiled in Rome.

> Dear Paco:
>
> I'm cooking in my kitchen in Rome. I remember when we cooked in your little house from Ciudad de la Paz, in Buenos Aires, eight or ten years ago. You liked to say little house. The Moor had died and we decided to eat and drink well one last time before taking him to his penultimate dwelling at the cemetery.
>
> Back then, a lot of people died from natural death. The Moor died from sickness, but it wasn't natural. He drank a lot, he had a head start of—about—12,000 liters of wine, and the moment

came in which he had to choose: an ascetic life, without alcohol, women nor tobacco; or a fast life. He chose the second one, for moral elegance . . .

And after that, they killed you. You were becoming deeper, happier and more human each time. I still think, since four or five years ago, that it would've been better that they sent you to Rome. Now you'd be cooking in your little house, remembering the Moor, remembering me, far, near.

I don't want to die in your place, although sometimes I would like to be in your place. What happened is that you told me one time that you'd live to be 80 years old, and I believed you. And I still believe you.[53]

On April 23, 1977, the Peronist Montonero Movement of Resistance was created to fight against the civic-military dictatorship. Gelman adhered to the organization. But a year later, under a new leadership, the organization resumed the militaristic strategy and announced a series of incomprehensible actions called "the strategic counteroffensive." The results were disastrous. An important number of militants were assassinated in a few days. Gelman, who didn't believe in the new leadership, began to disengage from the organization.

Since 1973, the Montoneros had committed a great number of very serious errors and had begun the exile. In addition, as it was considered a political and militaristic organization (and more militaristic than political), it adopted an absolute hierarchy and ridiculous attitudes. For example: At a certain moment, Firmenich[54] and company decided it was necessary to use a uniform. . . . The uniform consisted of a light blue shirt with small stars on the shoulders and a bright neck, like the Argentinian army. . . . On the other hand, in the beginning, the ranks in the organization were guerrilla-group type. But, while in exile, they started adopting the ranks of the Argentinian army. The most ridiculous thing was that they had to go places in uniform. They once had to meet in Madrid wearing the outfit, but since no one could walk the street in this manner, they brought their clothes to the meeting, and at the beginning and at the end, they had five minutes to change clothes.[55]

Despite the horrors that people suffered in Argentina, Gelman secretly returned to the country. In *Bajo la lluvia ajena (notas al pie de una derrota)* (*Under Someone Else's Rain [Footnotes of Defeat]*) he wrote the following:

XIX[56]

> I clandestinely returned to Buenos Aires in 1978. The city was beautiful.
>
> Or I should say, the most beautiful city under these days of May in which the autumn of Buenos Aires admits a light, a spring heat dying or to be born, one never knows.
>
> They have advised me that I should not walk downtown, that I should not frequent the sites that I used to frequent. Naturally: I walked downtown, through the sites that I used to walk. Who was going to recognize me?
>
> Wasn't Paco dead? Hadn't they kidnapped Rodolfo and Haroldo? Hadn't they killed Jote, Lino, Josefina, Dardo and Diana, perhaps?[57]

Gelman secretly returned to Argentina in October of 1976 and again in May of 1978. After this second trip, in an interview appearing in the weekly newspaper *Brecha* from Montevideo, Gelman said:

> . . . I understood that the exile was going to be long: the guerrilla organizations had been annihilated, the worker movement disjointed—although it opposed a resistance that was not very well organized—the political class supported the military regime by action or omission, and the Church blessed and smoothed the soul of murderers. A good part of society, without leadership from the resistance, lived in repression and a terror unknown

> in the history of the country. Another part of society swam into "easy money"[58] and practiced the "There must be a reason" cop-out.[59] The only real resistance, besides the worker, was The Mothers of Plaza de Mayo, and it still continued.

His second return coincided with his break with the Montoneros. Gelman returned after the 1978 Soccer World Cup; with a fake passport, he posed as a French journalist.

In the same interview, the journalist asked about the similarities between his life and some of the strategies used in his literary work.

> —It is fairly striking that you, who have invented various false poets (John Wendell, Sidney West, Julio Grecco) had created a French professor this time to hide your identity.

> —It was secretly my second return; I went into the country with a foreign passport and false identity. The following day, I took a taxi to go to meet a friend, and I got to chat with the driver without using the foreign accent necessary at other times. We were stopped at a military check point. A sergeant requested documents from me; I got out of the taxi as a precaution, since the taxi driver had heard me speak without an accent; I showed the sergeant my passport and, speaking in my corresponding foreign accent, I told him who I was supposed to be. The sergeant told me that they had found fake passports, and that mine would have to be verified. A lieutenant approached, and I asked him that I be allowed to go to "the closest police post" to talk with my ambassador. The lieutenant hesitated, at which point I complained like a stingy European that the taxi meter was still going and that others were waiting for me. Through all of this I was feeling strangely secure about the driver—who had also been asked for his documents and an explanation, and who had listened to me talk with a false accent—I wasn't going to be reported. The lieutenant let us go. I went back to the taxi; the car started; and the driver—who had red cheeks—looked at me through his rearview mirror and, after a long dense sigh, said to me, "What bad luck that

> they stopped us!" And later, "Do I take you to the same spot as you told me?" "Of course," I answered. "Yes," with a Buenos Aires accent, and that was that. I was indiscreet, but I was lucky. By that time, most taxi drivers were police informants.

The counteroffensive ordered by the Montoneros' leadership was delusional. For this reason, in addition to numerous others, Gelman decided to break with the organization.

Stage 4 (1979–2013) Without Political Party

In February of 1979, Gelman split from Montoneros because he disagreed with the military hierarchy that the organization had been following. Gelman chose to publicize the split in the daily French newspaper, *Le Monde*. Several days later, Montoneros accused him of treason and sentenced him to death.

> I only had contact with Galimberti[60] or with Firmenich, recently abroad. And abroad there is a very different type of practice. In the country, the contact was immediate, and a mistake was risky. But that didn't stop me from breaking with the Montoneros. For me, it was necessary to do it because of the craziness of the counter-offensive. Because they said, in 1977 or 1978, that the dictatorship was like a groggy boxer, and that it was only necessary to give it a slap to knock it down. Because risking the lives of many comrades in exile was stupid, and I couldn't agree with this. They didn't fire me, because I quit: They condemned me to death. I was condemned by both sides: The Triple A and the Montoneros. What a rare case! It was a sort of the happy hour for being condemned to death.[61]

The British novelist Graham Greene wrote an article for the newspaper the *Independent* portraying this deepening of the paradoxes of Argentina, with the poet convicted by the military and the leaders of the Montoneros, at the same time: ". . . So Mr. Gelman has achieved 2 death sentences."

The self-criticism of Gelman toward his own past with Montoneros is reflected in an interview published by Roberto Mero with the title "Conversaciones con Juan Gelman: Contraderrota, Montoneros, y la revolución perdida" ("Conversations with Juan Gelman: Counter-Defeat, Montoneros, and the Lost Revolution"). With pain, Gelman tells about the errors of the organization, which he labels "militaristic," "sectarian," "elitist," "unpopular," and "arrogant."

> At the base of this problem lies the focal theory of revolution, also known as focalism, which holds that it is the military struggle that drives the mass struggle, when it turns out that, in fact, the reality is quite the reverse. . . . If it is the organized masses who call for military action, then it would be the masses who should assume the task of self-defense. The military apparatus has to accompany them but should never dominate them.
>
> An example of such subordination of military actions to politics did exist in the first stage of the Peronist resistance. Let's say that one side, the Montoneros, experienced a process of political deterioration, moving in a militaristic direction similar to that of their enemy, copying even their enemy's rankings. . . . And when what prevails is the military, this leads only to a confrontation between armies and pieces of machinery, where it is evident that the Armed Forces are always going to win.[62]

All these issues and controversies can be found discussed in his poetry, especially in these two books: *Notas* (*Notes*) and *País que fue será* (*Country That Was Will Be*).

Notas, his twelfth book of poetry, contains twenty-seven poems written between August and October of 1979. The date is significant. It was six months after his formal split from Montoneros. In the following three excerpts, which appear in Notes VI, XIII, and XV, he expresses his feelings of contradiction and anger at the errors and arrogance of the organization.

> They defeated us/ by arrogant and death-blind[63]
> I am talking of the arrogance / the blindness /the

militaristic delirium of the management[64]
The mistakes/horrors of the national directions/ the
sectarianism/ the over-confidence/ the fatal militarism[65]

Notas condenses central themes that revolve around this rupture with its mixed feelings of guilt and anxiety. In "Nota VII," there is an example that reads:

I don't love you anymore/ fury
I don't love you anymore/ rage
you devastate my heart/
you make my heart blind to me

and I need that
clarity kiss me as
love where I love my end
as to start/ come here sadness[66]

At first, it's possible to read the annoyance and surfeit of an authorial voice that has been immersed in the senselessness of violence for many years: "no te quiero más/ rabia" (I don't love you anymore / rage.) This verse denounces the strategy of using violence against violence, hatred against the hatred of the dictators.

The contradictions in Gelman became more acute over time. With distance, things began to be seen another way. After the split, Gelman understood the madness that surrounded his actions in the guerrilla organization. Like many militants, Gelman never rejected the principles and reasons for which he had begun the fight, but he refuted the methods used that contradicted many of the organization's most fundamental principles. Gelman felt that objectives had begun to become more important than principles, and that militarism had become the only path. The absence of any other strategy makes one susceptible to a loss of the perspectives of class solidarity and national unity.

On the other hand, the book states feelings of guilt that closely relate to Gelman's condition at the time—as a survivor, and as someone in exile who is unable to stop disaster and death. Gelman had seen the worst of repression and had been an active part of the armed struggles. But unlike his partners, he had experienced life outside of danger, writing verses in Rome, Paris, and the paradisiacal Calella on the coast of Barcelona. The scenery, however, didn't matter. In fact, in these twenty-seven poems there are no geographic allusions. The sensations and airs that these texts breathe, which seem to swing between guilt and a sense of political obligation and responsibility to the fallen, are most important.

Note IV[67]

the fear of old age, does it grow old?
the fear of death, in death?
what am I doing with the thousands
of dead *compañeros*?

am I dying myself?
perhaps I'm afraid of them / beloved?
perhaps I'm afraid of you paco? / dear
like human happiness?

or do I envy them perhaps?
or do I envy them perhaps?
together as we were now
without any own and others' sufferings?

but why do I cry in you-
other pieces of my life?
perhaps I can cry finally?
can I finally mourn?

The impressions that these verses transmit are about fear, doubt, suffering, "propio y ajeno" (own and others' suffering), and pain. The lyrical group seemed destined to confront an elemental question: "¿qué estoy haciendo con los miles yo / de compañeros muertos?" (what am I doing with the thousands / of dead compañeros?) The responsibility of the poet-witness occupied the center of the debate. The names of those that were no longer present appear repeatedly, as well as friends and comrades of the struggle that died in battle against the dictatorship. Throughout the series, names mentioned countless times are Paco Urondo, Haroldo Conti, Rodolfo Walsh, El Jote, his son Marcelo Ariel, and other compañeros. The absences, paradoxically, are present in a constant and explicit manner. The absences that "no se callan" (don't remain silent) populate the conscience of the poet, as it is evident in "Nota XI," where the lyrical voice could barely resist attacks of the memory.

> memory lacks of reality / reality lacks of
> memory? / what to do with memory/ with reality
> in the middle of this defeat of soul?[68]

The absences of the partners and missing relatives began to increasingly weigh on Gelman's verses. The pain associated with not knowing where the *desaparecidos* were sharpened his perplexity. The vagueness and lack of certainty—they are the dead without corpses—hinders the duel: "matame vos los muertos" (you kill me my dead bodies).

Starting from the time he was forced to leave the homeland, the theme of memory occurred in all of Gelman's poetic works. In this and subsequent poems, as in this fragment of "Nota VII," one may observe a lyrical voice who admits his fragility and debates between a brutal, distant past and a present in exile.

> . . . come here sadness/
>
> you kill me my dead bodies that
> I backpack with all my soul /
> or finish killing them
>
> since the people continue/ like
> landscape or voice that doesn't remain silent /
> people who don't finish anymore[69]

Also notorious is the nonstandard use of verb tenses in relation to past circumstances: The past expresses in the future and the future through an imperfect past "... ya que moría mañana/ me moriré anteanoche" (... since I died tomorrow / I will die the night before last), writes Gelman in "Nota II." This new strategy stresses the confusion facing the immediate past. Another important element that appeared in "Nota IV" was the reference to blood:

> literally it rained blood/
> blood rained through my country
> from the veins the executioner cut off/
> from the heart that remembers them[70]

In one interview with Martín Prieto for *Revista 3 Puntos*, Prieto asks Gelman about the origin and meaning of the blood in his work. He responds with sarcasm: "It will be a metaphor of blood, man; what you want me to tell you? It was not lacking in this country, right?"

The permanent memory of what happened acted as a weight that prevented an exploration of other issues. The theme and style that persist throughout all the poems allow the book to maintain a certain homogeneity. There are constant allusions to the death of the compañeros that find equivalence in the formal level of speech and literary resources that he uses, like using anaphora (the repetition of words) and parallelism, the most frequently used figures of speech in the text, as we can observe in "Nota I."

> I will say your name time after time.
> ... I will show you my enraged heart,
> I will stomp on you mad with fury.
> I will kill you your bits.
> I will kill you one with paco
> ... I will kill you with my son in my hand.
>
> ... am going to kill you defeat.
> ... I am going to kill you/ I
> am going to kill you[71]

But pessimism does not permeate every aspect of Gelman's literary work, because there is also a place for redemption ("te voy a matar derrota") (I am going to kill you defeat), linking to a strong desire to begin a new life, far from the death and the madness: "amo mi acabar/ como empezar" (I love my end / as a start).

Notas then represented an end (of his awkward militancy and his military life) but also the assumption of a greater principle, with more freedom in his actions; a beginning where he need not obey questionable orders. Gelman expresses the desire to retrace his steps, return to the beginning and "viajar / viajar" (to travel / to travel), says "Nota V"; to reconsider what happened and to find new objectives and enthusiasm.

> . . . If I walked from anger in anger
> leaving from a dead entering
> to another dead or broken world /
> if I traveled in this way all these years /
>
> come closer/sadness/that
> such fury
> and such dead harbor get me cold, and
> I need to travel / to travel/[72]

The second moment aimed to inaugurate this new phase and, according to this desire to begin anew, Gelman started to see light, sun, and clarity where before he saw night, darkness, and horror. In the "Nota XIII"[73] we observe a permanent fluctuation between these opposite dualities. If in the first stanza he recovers what is positive *sol, alma, corazón,* and *memoria* (sun, soul, heart, and memory), in the second, he contrasts its opposites (*los errores, la derrota,* and *la soberbia/laceguera/el delirio*) (the errors, the defeat, and the arrogance/the blindness/the delirium). The third stanza returns to a state of light and flight, while in the fourth he asks if "se apagaron esos pedazos de sol ahora? / ¿ahora que los compañeros murieron?" (do these bits of sun shut off now? / now that the compañeros are dead?) The optimistic answer appears in the final stanza:

little sun that shut off like this/yet you light the night/in which we are looking at night/ towards the side where the sun rises

It is clear that in the end he attempts to be positive. It is as though Gelman gives birth to each one of these words with enormous effort and with the intention of opening the heavy door of redemption and alleviating hope. Latent optimism regarding the future always appears independent of the loneliness, sadness, and horror that hover over the texts of this phase. The blunt end of the "Nota III" shows this new perspective: "empújenlos al triunfo" (push them to triumph).

Also in "Nota XVII" that begins alluding to the fall ("entre otras cosas / la derrota") (among other things / defeat), to finish with a warning ("para seguir buscando luz") (to continue looking for light), one can find optimism. This happens again in the "Nota XVIII" that begins with the outline of the fatal landscape ("estamos vivos / entre compañeros/ caídos por delación o combate") (we are alive / among *compañeros*/ fallen by denunciation or combat) to gradually advance toward a bright statement that would seem to be inspired by their own deeds: "rostros fosforescentes vemos como astros / subir / volar / callar a pedacitos / lámparas de la ciega libertad / que reventó ojos amados / para que salga toda luz" (phosphorescent faces we see as stars / that climb/fly / that keep quiet by bits / lamps of the blind freedom / that burst beloved eyes / so that all light goes out).

País que fue será, his twenty-sixth book of poems, published in 2004, expressed the same enthusiasm for a new beginning seen in *Notas*. The text proposed a type of generational game. The title announces two realities, a crisscross between two generations. They are the generation that belongs to Gelman, his compañeros, and dead poets, and the young generation that will come. It is as if Gelman suggested that the new generations will populate and fill the streets of the republic again, protesting against injustice; which will return to write and sing, which will resume the dreams of a better world. It was as if Gelman predicted the day in which the legacy of the generation of the '70s would be inevitably recovered for the country's future generations. In April of 2008, Gelman and journalist Horacio Verbitsky reflected about the crossing over:

—Today you can say *País que fue será*, but 20 years ago you saw a country that you were afraid would never be again. You had idealized your return. For you, returning was the moment of truth and justice; you were going to reveal who killed Marcelo. You met with a very gray reality. Nevertheless, over the years you achieved from Mexico an impact on Argentina life greater than what you idealized when you were in Paris. Only someone capable of generating a reality of one's self can get it, someone very great.

—What Menem did was terrible, the sale of the country, in addition to the impunity of the pardons; the disaster of De La Rúa; the recovery that began with Néstor Kirchner. I lived as if from afar but closely.

Gelman seemed to anticipate the winds of change that began to blow in the region after 2001. As if the title of the book and that little warning weren't clear enough, Gelman began the book with a quote from French medieval poet Guillaume de Poitiers, which pointed in the same direction: "El paraíso perdido nunca estuvo atrás. Quedó adelante." (The lost paradise never was behind. It was ahead.) In an interview with Vicente Muleiro and Eduardo Pogorites, Gelman explained the significance of this quote.

—In *País que fue será* the theme is that Paradise is always ahead. For your generational experience, it is a strong example of optimism.

—Yes, "the paradise was ahead." If you want, you can read it as a hopeful expectation, I think one can. Finally, hope is the last thing one lost.

As philosopher Dardo Scavino said in his article titled "Juan Gelman: la revolución es un fuego eterno" ("Juan Gelman: The Revolution is an Eternal Flame"), Gelman's return to the past to revisit the painful years of death and repression corresponded to a yearning to reveal the mysteries of the past while working to dispel them.

Recalling the past does not mean committing a pious act of idolization of one's heroes. To remember the past—the triumphs and the defeats, the loves and the deceptions, the

> enthusiasms and the treachery, the battles and the tortures—means to find in each one of these incidents, in everything that could be done and written—from Sappho down to Contursi,[74] passing by Baudelaire or Vallejo—the secret index that points to the redemption or to the mystery of time that is to come.[75]

País que fue será became the end of a journey and a poetic summary that went from the past to the future and from lost dreams to hope. Against all predictions, including "those things that did not occur," the journey goes from "el porvenir/ atrás" (the future/ behind), as the poet said in "Flautas" ("Flutes"), as if all times would coexist in the present in his poetry.

A Thousand Pages of Exile

For Juan Gelman, the ups and downs of presence and absence, the period inside and outside his country, in legal limbo, defined his literary production and altered his own writing practice. Like many of the committed intellectuals of his time, Gelman had to abandon his country in an abrupt manner. The Montoneros leadership thought that, with the political conditions that had led to the death of Juan Perón, Gelman—as an active member of the guerrilla organization—would be more useful to the cause if he were absent from the country. That rationale was how his move was decided.

The man responsible for communicating the news to Gelman was poet Francisco "Paco" Urondo, also part of the guerilla group. As Gelman remembered it, they shared an undercover house in Constitución, a neighborhood of the city of Buenos Aires.

One afternoon Gelman opened the door of his house and found Urondo, who immediately made a gesture toward the ground with his right thumb, as was done by the Roman emperors. The decision had been made. Among other reasons, death threats from the Triple A during the Isabel Martínez de Perón administration obliged the poet to abandon the country and go to Rome.

What initially seemed to be a temporary exile lasted thirteen years. The exile defined, in a definite way, one of the themes of his poetics, i.e., his method of seeing and speaking about the world.

Soon after arriving in Italy, he worked in the news agency Inter Press Service, where he was responsible for the management of a network of Latin American correspondents. With the passing of years, he juggled work with the news and work in translation. During the '80s he was hired as a translator for the United Nations, after winning second place in an arduous competition that included more than three hundred candidates. He then worked for the different organizations of the institution, including UNESCO and FAO.

During his initial political activity in Rome, Gelman spearheaded what would become the first international public declaration of opposition to the Argentinian dictator by securing signatures from government leaders. The paid press release was published in the French newspaper *Le Monde* with the signatures of Françoise Mitterrand, Olof Palme, Austrian chancellor Bruno Kreisky, Willy Brandt, Danish prime minister Anker Henrik Jørgensen, Italian jurist Francesco de Martino, Mario Soares, and the British Labor Party member Ron Hayward, among others.

Gelman recalled details of a story from when he met with Austrian prime minister Bruno Kreisky to seek his advocacy:

> The person in charge of foreign relations of the Social Democrats called me to the party headquarters, where Kreisky was the Secretary General. Kreisky read the declaration and told me that he could not sign it because, given his investiture, it infringed on international principles. I told him that I had not asked him for a signature as the Prime Minister but as the leader of the party. He laughed and said, "But Mr. Gelman, please." I told him, "It is alright Mister Prime Minister, I only want you to remember what happened with León Blum and the Spanish Civil War." I got up, took the raincoat that had been put up on a hook, and with a savage fury I called the elevator. Behind me the person responsible for the foreign affairs of the party came running and told me: "Kreisky is going to sign."[76]

Gelman's reference to the Spanish Civil War was convenient and particularly irritating because Blum, as prime minister of France, declared in 1936 the neutrality of his country, in spite of the conflict that affected Spain. This was the unconstitutional uprising of Francisco Franco's troops that launched the Spanish Civil War. With this decision, the Second Spanish Republic remained isolated in its peninsula without assistance from France or an escape through it. This painful memory undoubtedly mobilized Kreisky.

Gelman's pilgrimage in exile included residency in more than twenty cities in at least eight different countries. After Italy, Gelman lived in Nicaragua, Spain, France, Switzerland, the United States, Argentina, and, finally, Mexico.

With the triumph of the Nicaraguan Revolution in 1979, Gelman established himself in Managua and began to collaborate in the recently founded news agency Nueva Nicaragua, reliant upon the Nicaraguan government. He resolutely supported the Nicaraguan government and the struggle of the Farabundo Martí Liberation Front in El Salvador during times of insurgency in Central America. In his long poem, "Crónicas" ("Chronicles"), he reviewed the history of the American Tom Thumb and concluded:

> the Salvadorians are speaking with eternity/ they climb
> the sky and write 'down with misery' / they sew their
> heart to the bells/ in order to fly/ to fly

The Difficulties of Writing from Exile

During the first five years of his long period of exile, Gelman could not bring himself to write. He found himself impeded by various circumstances. Despite the fact that he was exiled, far from harassment and real risk of death, the new circumstances were completely disconcerting: The language was different, his routine and political activity were disrupted, his family and friends were not present, and he could not appeal to the code he shared with his public and his compatriots. In an interview with Ana Laura Peréz, published in *Clarín* during May of 1980, he said:

> . . . exile is a cow that can give poisoned milk, at least to those few that seem to feed in this way. . . . The need to self-destruct and the need to survive quarrel like two brothers driven crazy.

Among the numerous anecdotes that the poet remembered from his first years in Rome, there is one that perfectly captured the state of general confusion in which the exile lived during those first years. In the following memory, dark humor and an ironic analysis of his own misfortune were mixed:

> . . . a Sunday, in Rome, at three in the afternoon, I go to visit a friend and proceed towards the Coliseum, that resembled the River Plate soccer stadium, only it is smaller. . . . the issue is that it was Sunday, summer, and many people were visiting, vendors were there selling ice cream, balloons, pipes and all of that, and suddenly I hear this whistle and I said to myself "the match has begun . . . " but it turned out that it was the whistle of the guard that was chasing away some kids that ran into the ruins in the center.[77]

In addition to becoming accustomed to this new environment, Gelman had to struggle with a problem that in his case was vital: the language. Initially, the Italian language seemed to generate a noise that impeded him from feeling inspired as he was with the Spanish spoken in Argentina. In an interview published in *La Maga*, Gelman says:

> The Italian language is very sweet. It is very smooth. It has many short cuts that allow you to lie down and rest. . . . For my work, I felt this every time Italian was in the ear, and this bothered me, because the load of my obsessions, that which I wanted to express, had more fury than relaxation.

In order to resist the linguistic trap, Gelman began to write a series of sonnets in Roman slang with a pornographic tone:

> The men of the agency where I worked were dying of laughter. I had invented a personality, the Nono, that said the most terrible things.[78]

Another substantial issue was related to the nature of the writing. He was far away from his audience, his people, the places that he tended to frequent; the words, expressions, and experiences that led him to begin his profession. For the exiled writer, this is a great loss, since his way of life, his way of relating to the rest of the social body, is through writing. If all of that could not be shared, it is very difficult to write. This is exemplified by the large number of writers who decided to permanently abandon writing during and after exile. Of the forty exiled Argentinian writers in Mexico, for instance, only eleven published books while in exile. Gelman mentions a memory of writer Leopold Marechal:

> Marechal told me once that when he left the country he could not write, since he needed to be amongst his people, to hear them talk in order to continue writing. Even though this is a general formula, I don't see why it has to apply to everyone. In my personal case, this situation greatly impacts my work, especially my poetry, because the most essential material to my work is the word, the colloquial speech of the people. But, I repeat, that is the result of a personal matter.[79]

Another of the obstacles that the exile was forced to face dealt with the continuation of literary practice. This relates to the essence of writing as it is done in a highly specialized language, with innuendos, gestures, and suppositions. The writer constructed his work according to a completely well-defined public, which in exile is distanced in a way that can be irreparable, thus provoking writer's "block," "contamination," or the direct interruption of the work.

The cutoff in these cases makes the situation twice as difficult. The author does not merely find himself unable to be in his country with his people; he cannot develop the work for which he is educated and through which he expresses the majority of his worries and longings. The work loses its continuity. To attempt resuming it outside the scope in which Gelman was thinking and feeling was not just tedious work; at times it was impossible because the benchmark was different.

Among all these disadvantages that the exile had to suffer, another important phenomenon was occurring. The everyday experiences that the exile was having far from his country of origin were different from those of the people who remained. Every political, historical, social, and cultural event in the exiles' countries while they were outside those countries was not lived in the same way as by those who remained. On the other hand, those who remained in the country did not know the experiences lived by the exiles abroad. This produced a sort of mutual distancing which widened the crack of isolation between those who left and those who remained. As a result, every year of separation increased the exile's isolation. Paul Illie, who studied the consequences of exile during the Francisco Franco regime, analyzed it as follows:

> . . . the residents (referring to those who were not exiled) will develop certain cognitive forms in social conditions that are thoroughly disassociated from the realities of emigration.[80]

Perhaps that was the reason why, after thirteen years of living away from his country, Gelman could not return to live in Argentina. Neither was Argentina the same that it was thirteen years before, nor was he the same after so much exile and isolation.

After five years, Gelman appeared to conclude that although poetry did not change the world, the world could not silence poetry. With this mutual impossibility, silence was unthinkable. After these first years of silence, Gelman began writing again until his last days.

Theodor Adorno's "Education after Auschwitz," first presented as a radio lecture on April 18, 1966, under the title "Pädagogik nach Auschwitz," considered it an impossible task to write well when one speaks of Auschwitz. The idea gave rise to a presupposition: the horror could not be described, nor could it be a poetic theme. Nevertheless, in the speech for the Juan Rulfo Prize for Latin American and Caribbean Literature that Gelman received on November 26, 2000, he was allowed to disagree.

> Theodor Adorno once uttered an unhappy phrase: He affirmed that it was not possible to write poetry after Auschwitz. He confused himself; and then there is the work of Paul Celan that disputes it, or the work of Kenzaburo Oé, after Hiroshima and Nagasaki. For years, I thought the error of Adorno consisted in an omission, that he missed an "as before," that one could not write poetry as before Auschwitz, as before Hiroshima and Nagasaki, as before the Argentinian genocide.

Marks of Exile in Gelman's Work

This first period of literary interruption was a troubling time that extended for five years, after which Gelman began to recover the lost time and to write profusely. After 1979 and during the next nine years of exile that remained, he published the following thirteen books of poems: *Comentarios* (*Commentaries*); *Citas* (*Citations*); *Notas* (*Notes*); *Carta abierta* (*Open Letter*); *Si dulcemente* (*If Sweetly*); *Bajo la lluvia ajena (notas al pie de una derrota)* (*Under Someone Else's Rain [Footnotes of Defeat]*); *Hacia el sur* (*Toward the South*); *La junta luz* (*The Junta Light*); *Eso* (*That*); *Com/posiciones* (*Com/positions*); *Anunciaciones* (*Annunciations*); and *Carta a mi madre* (*Letter to My Mother*).

In this return to words, we discover the continuation of struggle. To return to poetry is neither an act of reconciliation for Gelman, nor an acceptance of the new situation, but a sign of resistance. The production of this period portrayed the profound impact that isolation, exile, the end of his militancy, pain, and love made in his life.

With the intention of recognizing traces of exile in his poetry, we will examine five of his most important poetry books of the time: *Hechos, Citas, Notas, Hacia el sur,* and *Anunciaciones.*

Hechos, Gelman's ninth poetry book, is the first book that was finished in exile. It was published in 1980, and it recounts the story of his exit. In this first book during exile, he gives evidence without disguising deception and loss. Voices of defeat appear, but they are no longer those of residents of far points of the planet, as suggested in his previous book, *Relaciones.* Instead they are voices of his own inner circle, including Haroldo Conti ("haroldo triste") (sad haroldo); Dardo Dorronsoro ("dardo fusilado") (executed dardo); Francisco "Paco" Urondo ("no está paquito") (paquito is not here); Mario Lorenzo Koncurat, known as "El Jote" ("el jote de ojos altos") (jote of raised eyes); Rodolfo Walsh, and many others. There is also a place for lesser-known activists. Gelman mentions many other names, like those of "Marcos," "Diana," "Quique," "la cabezona" (The Stubborn One) "Huaqui," "Miguel," "Roque," "el pata" (The Buddy), "Gaby," "Pedro," and "Antonio." All are included in the poem "Ausencias" ("Absences"). The title undoubtedly verifies this loss:

paquito is not here / son of the memory / and neither
is marcos of the language filled with amazement/
and neither transparent, defenseless diana/ nor
brown quique/ the tender stubborn one/ the gentle
huaqui of iron/ nor sad haroldo/ nor executed dardo/
nor miguel that fixed the night with his eyes of a
cat/nor roque in his common vest/ nor the crazy
buddy/ nor gaby that had a light in her face/ pedro/
antonio from the table with god/ jote of raised eyes/
they left fighting. . . . [81]

The climate of terror within Argentina that appeared to have no end led him to write a poem in which he imagined his own death. "Muertes" ("Deaths"), probably the second poem that was written in exile, speculated on how he would die. His death was the aim of the three organizations that condemned him to death: the military junta, the right-wing Peronist paramilitary organization Triple A, and the left-wing Peronist guerrilla Montoneros:

> I don't want to see anything else of that death . . . especially the day of my death.[82]

The worldly moment was important and marked a change in the poetics of the writer. As we will see in his later works, an insistent emphasis of the theme of tragedy would begin to increasingly occupy his literary concerns and obsessions. If the earlier poems interrogated love, poetry, and the revolution, in this tragic instance—where all is lost—death would acquire a specific and unique weight.

With *Hechos,* a change in Gelman's formal work began. The change was reflected through marks that denoted caesura, a continuous use of double vertical lines in the verses. These caesuras provoke a break in the cadence of every verse, fracture reading, and create intermittent rhythmic periods. Gelman achieved what Cuban poet Lezama Lima admired in a writer: the capacity to destroy and recreate the language at the same time one did this to one's own life. "Descansos" ("Breaks"), the poetry written as a tribute to Paco Urondo, is one of the texts that provides evidence of this strategy of incompletion and interruption:

under which tree/on top of which tree/around
which tree/ francisco urondo appears?/[83]

Facing the difficult task of identifying the theme of horror, those vertical bars in his verse function as if they are cracks or holes where the author seems to place that which was left on the other side of the Atlantic: the missing companions and lost illusions. These unexpected caesuras appeared to be the first "interruptions" that suggested that cuts were abrupt and unexpected, as were exile and death.

Citas, the eleventh book of poems by Gelman, written in Rome between November and December of 1979, allude specifically to the texts of Saint Teresa of Ávila (also called Saint Teresa of Jesús), and continue the spiritual writings and mysticism of *Comentarios*, his previous poetry book.

The thematic core appeared on the dedication page: "to my country," an evocative country that appeared far away and that the poet could not name. It turned out that he did not mention any concrete place in Argentinian geography, as if the poet could not name just what needed to be said.

Beside the use of bars, there are various formal marks that seem especially present. One of them is the use of what we refer to as "antithetical neologism," where Gelman created new vocabulary through the union of words of conflicting meaning, like *solombra* (sunshade), *vosmí* (youme), *muerevida* (dieslife), etc. This collection also includes a series of rhetorical questions that sometimes alluded to impossible answers: "soul that you take me/ where does it go?/ it goes?"[84]

Adjectives and nouns with their gender and number changed are among other included innovative methods. Verbs partnered with unexpected nouns also appear: "me dejás dejádome"[85] (you leave me abandoning me), "sangre que me sangrás"[86] (blood that you bleed me), "goce de este gozo"[87] (enjoyment of this joy).

In this book, Gelman appears to play with the impossibilities of writing in Castilian Spanish while in Rome. That is why he decided to create what is known as paronomasia, the method of placing terms of similar sound with different significance near one another, generating a strange toxicity in his diction:

ama mía/ es decir rama que me amás[88]

(soul of mine/ that is to say a branch that loves me)

Citas is the text of a multivoiced encounter, a tumult of verbal twists and languages in constant overlap.

Notas, the twelfth book of poetry by Gelman, written between August and October of 1979, has a predominant poetic strategy: The book is full of parallel structures with the connecting conjunction *ni* (nor). This is a strategy that does no more than promote the setting of the scene of exclusion and exile:

> . .. neither heart nor nothing// nor the word nothing//
> nor the word heart/.[89]

Verses with meanings that seem interchangeable also appear in the book, as if Gelman would like to test and approve terms that were not initially conceived as such. Words like *soul, fury, death,* and *sadness* seem to function as correlative terms:

> the fury that pursued the soul// the sadness that pursued
> the fury// the death that pursued the sadness.[90]

As in *Hechos,* Gelman promoted the extensive use of verses with caesuras to express the interruption that signified exile. In many cases, the first verse of a certain stanza was a subordinate clause of the previous stanza's last verse, challenging the regular order of a reading:

> . . . by a field of broken comrades/ which do not
> dampen the twilight. . . . finally still/ without fear/ to
> death/ corpses.[91]

Hacia el sur, Gelman's sixteenth volume of poems, was written between 1981 and 1982. In this new poetic proposal, the author makes a decisive denunciation of the horror characterizing the dictatorship's actions. He uses an explicit method, also appealing to a series of formal resources, including the use of an irony that is simultaneously acidic and tender, putting the drama of going into exile and the complexity of the editing job in the scene:

> when jean (hans) arp (harp) when hans harp died . . .
> giving the fact that johnny harp has died[92]

Gelman used some of these methods, including unusual metaphors, to force readers to contemplate the increasing perplexity in which he lived as an exile:

> "her love is a comb that goes combing through here/"[93]

or

> "there is an eye of fire sitting at my table."[94]

In second place, concepts appear changing their traditional definitions. In this example, he references celestial angels:

> the angels begin to furiously scratch themselves/ with
> hooves that grew on them.[95]

What follows is the interruption of a monotonous tone of voice that confronts the reality of exile and banishment:

> I am going to burn this sadness in the afternoon/ as a
> heap with which to scare away the ages[96]

The presence of disappointment within the hostile and external world of exile appears as inevitable. His anguish demanded immediate expression. His hand could not stop the impulse to tell how it felt to be expelled far from home:

> why are you saddened/ my little hand/ why do you
> crackle in the darkness without allowing me to sleep?
> . . . why do you rain/hand?[97]

Finally, he presents opposing images, giving the sensation of chaos and a lack of control, where angels appeared together with phantoms, torture together with hope, body with spirit, beauty with insanity, the sun with the moon, dictatorship with revolution, enjoyment with fear, right with left, heaven with hell, and ultimately, dreams with death.

The secrecy of *Anunciaciones*, his twenty-first book of poems, written in 1985 when Gelman still found himself an exile, manifests itself through the complexity of methods that Gelman used in previous texts. We find orthographic violations in conjugated verbs such as *rompidas* (broken) and *escribido* (written) as well as incredible semantic constructions, such as, "¡lujosa de odio y soledad!"[98] (the luxuriousness of hate and solitude) and "¡cerraste lo gorrión con tus alejaciones!"[99] (you close the sparrow with your separation). Poetry, in Gelman's exile period, is a vehicle to contemplate himself and evaluate concrete facts, knowing that it is autonomous and behaves according to its own logic and rules.

The Unsolved Mysteries of Exile

Closely related to the formal and stylistic devices of the preceding section, Gelman began writing a long series of questions that keep accumulating, with varied intentions.

In *Relaciones*, his eighth poetry book written before his exile between 1971 and 1973, questions in his poetry maintain a symmetric and balanced structure. In the majority of cases, verses align themselves in the following way: four verses affirm, then four question; finally, four deny or come to affirm, as is the case in "Necesidades" ("Necessities"), "Situaciones" ("Situations"), "Defectos" ("Defects"), and "Preguntas" ("Questions").

The main goal of this strategy could have been related to the technique that Socrates called Maieutic, a dialectic mechanism of approaching the truth by asking successive questions. Gelman's idea, from my perspective, is to guide the reader through the questions in order for that reader to find his own answers. Through this series of concatenated questions, Gelman intended to direct readers to a poetic revelation by their own devices and means, their own intuitive and inductive reasoning. This Socratic mode of inquiry intends to bring a person's latent ideas into clear consciousness.

The etymology of the term *Maieutic* comes from the Greek definition of *midwife*. The tiered structure of the questions posed by Gelman demands different levels of understanding so that the reader is "giving birth to," with a great deal of effort—as does a midwife. Because readers complete this poetic circuit based on their personal experiences, this is also known as the theory of reminiscence.

In "Preposiciones" ("Prepositions"), for example, this strategy pretends to "awaken" the latent knowledge in the memory of the reader, so that the reality of the poem is completed and enriched by the reader's experiences:

> where the female worker in love went?/ did she go to
> the air?/ the female worker of the word died/ To which
> primrose path did she go?[100]

In the sequence of questions every element of the assembly essentially relates to the previous and subsequent elements. It is clearly for this reason that Gelman chooses the title of the piece. *Relaciones* means a new reading strategy that links all of the poems, as if they could be read as a single indivisible composition. This is implied in "Relaciones," the poem that inspired the title of the book:

> that stone. Does it have to do with him?
> the man across the street from the shoe store. Does he

have to do with him?
the millions of chinese indians angolans that he doesn't
know. Do they have to do with him?
God's strange little pest saint anthony. Does it have to
do with him?

that stone has to do with him
that man across the street from the shoe store has to do
with him
the millions of chinese indians angolans that he doesn't
know have to do with him
God's strange little pest saint anthony has to do with
him[101]

Disparate objects and distant elements, apparently unconnected, end up being related and associated with man, other living beings, and other objects. All have to do with all. Everything is interrelated. There are no individual programs; there are neither partial nor biased readings. The relations are extensive, in time and in space.

However, in *Hechos*, his first book while in exile, questions do not maintain their anterior structure. In some cases, the poem is one big question, as in "Descansos" ("Rests") and "Abrigos" ("Shelters"); in others, there are no questions, although the tone is inquisitive, as it happens in "Héroes" ("Heroes") and in "Sábanas" ("Sheets").

In other compositions, the questions appear isolated or inter-circled in an irregular form as is the case of "Cantos" ("Songs"): "rugiendo en mi país? / ¿estás paquito ahí o" (roaring in my country? / are you paquito here or). The interrupted question will continue in the second stanza.

At the end, questions continue to accumulate, finishing with one word, as in the following cases: " . . . ¿descansan// tus huesitos?/ en guerra?// ¿en paz?/ ¿agüita?/ ¿nunca?"[102] (do your little bones/ rest// in war?// in peace?/ little water?/ never?)

Hechos signals a paradigm shift regarding the proposal made in *Relaciones*. In *Relaciones* we observed a fragile poetic conviction manifested through questions and personal responses. However, in *Hechos,* a higher degree of confusion and uncertainty is evident, where there are no responses, only questions and fragments.

Merchants of Exile

During the year 1980, with the perspective of five years of exile already completed, Gelman begins to observe speculative attitudes of people who look to profit from the painful theme of exile. In *Bajo la lluvia ajena (notas al pie de una derrota),* Gelman's fifteenth book of poems that was written in Rome in May of that year, three poetic moments explicitly appear where he questions those "Vampires of Exile":

> Exile would be more bearable without so many professors of exile, sociologists, poets of exile, criers of exile, students of exile, professionals of exile, good souls with a little scale in their hands weighing the more and the less, the residual, the division of the distances, the 2x2 of this misery.[103]

The new merchandise gives good profits to the merchants of exile. They are oblivious to the substantial and complex issues of living far from home. More than this, they are oblivious to the hand-to-hand combat that hundreds of thousands of Latin Americans face for surviving every day in the mud where the cruelest dictatorships rule. These professionals of exile only report the echo of an unsubstantial issue that they don't fully understand. They remain on the surface of exile and, therefore, on the surface of the unsaid and unfeeling, the meaninglessness. Most certainly, as pointed out by Gelman, they are moved by power and academic prestige. In the poem "XV" the accusation takes form:

> When some Europeans realize the business opportunity that represents the Latin American exile, they strangely change their faces, they hesitate, they go pale as if the fears of childhood had returned. Later they recover themselves and their seriousness, they recognize that solidarity is necessary and, above all, mutually convenient. Of the blood of many compañeros they will write an article or two, they would get some academic chair, a salary. Which is irrelevant.[104]

In the same poem, Gelman remembers the total opposite attitude of the famous poet Francisco "Paco" Urondo:

> Paco Urondo died for the happiness of millions who wanted to have a decent quality of life. He did not aspire to write or gain prestige with his fight. Of the remains of Paco eats a raven that is now publishing anthologies and giving lectures about Paco at the European university of B.[105]

The critics against the merchants of exile open the door to more globalized visions. Gelman's European residence appears to have expanded his frontiers and created new interpretations of the conquest and colonization of the Americas:

> Who said that culture does not smell? // I stroll through Rome, Paris, and they are very beautiful. On Via del Corso and Bulmish I suddenly catch a smell of Tainos devoured by Andalusian dogs, of Ona ears mutilated, of Aztecs melting into Lake Tenochtitlan, of the little Inca broken in Potosí, of Querandí, Araucan, Congo, Carabalí, enslaved, massacred// You don't smell old, Europe// You smell of double standards, the one that assassinates, the one that is assassinated// Centuries have passed and the beauty of the vanquished still rots your brow.[106]

But the questioning is not directed solely at the indolent Europeans. It also includes some of his nationals who never stopped profiting from the unfortunate situation of many exiles:

> I read the newspapers of the old times. In *La Opinión*—where I worked at some point, that at some time I founded—an intellectual companion of the left (ex-companion or ex-leftist) added his paid voice to the propaganda of the dictatorship. The newspaper now belongs to the military dictators. My ex-companion or ex-leftist as well// I try to remember his name, but I don't remember it. He was a short-story writer, or something like that, like his wife, who shitted on Rosa Luxemburg's ideas from leftist positions. She had a leftist anus that would not have prevented her from evacuating the daily military ration.[107]

In one of the scenes of the Oscar-winning movie *The Official Story*, the Spanish father doubts his son (a new rich, interpreted by Héctor Alterio, who benefited from the dictatorship).

> The whole country went down, only the sons of bitches, the robbers, the accomplices and my older son went up.

The parallel is relevant. Gelman doubts the intellectual honesty of some of his ex-companions.

Finally, it is worth mentioning that the book, written in a prose format, contains only two notes written in verse: notes "V" and "XV." The remainder of the text utilizes a plain and narrative language. Lexical innovations previously used no longer appear. Perhaps this absence is related to the characteristics of this book. In this new composition, Gelman feels ready for the first time to discuss in detail the extent and consequences of his exile.

Late Exile, Arrest Warrant, and Democracy

In 1983, with the final stretch of the dictatorship and the new democracy already functional, Gelman decided to return to Argentina. However, he was thwarted when Judge Juan Miguel Guillermo Pons reinstated an arrest warrant based on an illicit association, regarding Gelman's participation in Montoneros. The judge specifically alluded to a conference of Montoneros in Rome in 1977 in which Gelman had participated.

After three years of not appearing before the judge, Gelman was declared in contempt of court and an international warrant was issued for his arrest. Reacting to Gelman's order of capture, a group of Latin American writers objected to Gelman's prosecution. Among those in solidarity were Augusto Roa Bastos, Mario Vargas Llosa, Eduardo Galeano, Octavio Paz, Gabriel García Márquez, Juan Carlos Onetti, and the Italian Alberto Moravia. In Argentina, journalist Horacio Verbitsky and the leader of the Christian Democratic Party, Carlos Auyero, solicited exemption from prison for Juan Gelman on the last day of the year.

Gelman remained in exile during the first five years of democracy, from 1983 to 1988. During those five years, Gelman wrote two books,

Eso and *Anunciaciones*, closely related to the kind of legal limbo in which he was trapped.

Eso includes twenty texts written in Paris between 1983 and 1984 and is Gelman's eighteenth book of poems. It is a work, he said, that was produced while packing the bags to undertake his final return. However, the return is delayed:

> I was packing my bag when a friend called me and told me not to return since Judge Pons had opened a case against me. If I went back, they would capture me. Then I stayed. It took more than four years before I could return. I was upset, of course, but I did not say that I would never return to Argentina. I don't hate Argentina. They are the military who are confused, believing that they are the owners of Argentina. I'll never confuse military with Argentina.[108]

If *Relaciones* and *Hechos* portrayed the forced departure from Argentina and the beginning of a long exile, this new book would pose a paradoxical situation. On the one hand is this kind of legal limbo in which the poet exists: his exile continues despite the end of the dictatorship. On the other hand is the latent and imminent possibility of return.

Over time, the hope for a quick resolution of the legal situation becomes hopeless. The legal irresolution imposes its time and prevents the return. Gelman experienced this exhausting process throughout 1984 and writes the heartbreaking poem, "Los ilusos" ("The Dreamers") in response to excessive initial optimism and a democracy with many pending issues:

The Dreamers[109]

> Hope fails many times, pain ever. That is why
> some believe that a known pain is better than an
> unknown pain.
> They believe that hope is an illusion. They are the
> dreamers of pain

The legal limbo is also clearly represented in "Alrededor del cual" ("Around Which"), where a speaker shows the impossibility of defining the word *alma* (soul). Eight definitions of words derived from the word *alma* are included; but there is no specific mention of this word: "almiar is," "almea is," "almarada is," "almanta is," "almez is," "almagre is," "almona is," "almorta is." The word *alma* can be surrounded, fenced, intuited, but in no way expressed or fully defined. The narrator roams around the core concern, as do the judges who are delaying decisions on Gelman's procedural situation.

Regarding this situation, Belgian critic Geneviève Fabry says in her book, titled *Las formas del vacío: La escritura del duelo en la poesía de Juan Gelman* (*Forms of Emptiness: The Dual Writing in Juan Gelman's Poetry*), that this strategy is "As if Gelman sought how to say *that* (*eso*), how to approach again *that* which has not been said."[110]

The other book of poems that accounts for this situation is *Anunciaciones*, Gelman's twenty-first book. The fifty-eight poems that make up this volume, primarily written in Paris during 1985, take the form of a violent interrogation. Following a mysterious voice in the second person, a battery of questions unfolds that remains throughout the composition. All of these questions require clarification on issues that seem inconceivable, "¿será posible que no mares?[111] / ¿que no se parta en puertos tu ojo roto?"[112] ("will it be possible that you don't drown? / that your broken eyes don't split into ports?"). The innumerable "will it be possible" questions included in this composition clearly reflect his exile situation: How is it possible that four years after the end of the dictatorship, Gelman and many other poets remain in the ostracism of exile? How is it possible?

What is truly innovative in this production appears with a high and exasperated tone. Unlike the maieutic strategy previously used, Gelman addresses this new stage with shouted responses among exclamation marks, creating a much more radicalized and hermetic tone: "¡han desollado al roedor pensante!"[113] (they have flayed the thinking rodent!) There are no longer only questions, but also enigmatic and forceful statements.

The lyrical voice, which feels trapped in this Argentine postdictatorial world, bursts with anger and injustice. This contradiction between his syntax and exclamations fills his poetry, with images like "llaves sin puertas" (keys without doors) and "espejos que nada reflejan" (mirrors that reflect nothing). The questioning of bureaucratic political organizations is also critical and present with images like this: "comité central del parpadeo"[114] (Flicker Central Committee).

The Endless Exile

On January 7, 1988, the Federal Court of the City of Buenos Aires annulled the resolution of Judge Miguel Guillermo Pons, exempting Gelman of imprisonment, on his own recognizance. The writer returned to Argentina in June, 1988, after thirteen years of exile. Gelman said:

> In my case, returning signifies the reunion with emptiness. My memory reconstructed its gaps, encountering unexpected presences, like the presence of fear, of what happened and what has been forgotten.[115]

With his return, a stage of pain that seemed insurmountable was partially closed. The separated parts no longer fit perfectly as before, because neither was Gelman the same as when he left, nor was the country the same as when it was abandoned. Gelman continued:

> What I noticed after so many years of exile are the changes in the country, and, of course, my own changes. One changes his condition in exile. It was a period of much meditation and reflection, not only of political ideologies. There were people who had pictures, in my opinion, quite simplistic about the exile: exile has a good side and a bad side. The thing went far beyond: the culture of the people, languages, habits . . . all those things were changing the way we look at the world. All countries have their own smells and tastes. Argentina has its own, and I still can recognize them, despite my changes and the changes in the country. I did not want to make pilgrimages, but my responsibilities forced me to visit many places, cafes where I used to go, the neighborhood where I grew up, the high school where I studied, houses where friends of mine lived, like Paco Urondo, who is dead. I walked by the neighborhood where my son and his wife were kidnapped. The absences that I noticed the most were the absences of those people who are no longer alive, and my own absence in relation to those years and those people. It is as if a circle closed at the same point where it started, and as if

> all those years in exile suddenly did not exist. I was afraid to meet with the piece of myself that remained and stayed here, in a country that is no longer as it was then.[116]

Mexico, His Final Residence

After an intense pilgrimage, Gelman established his permanent residence in Mexico on January 19, 1989. This decision had to do with two fundamental issues. On the one hand, it was related to his own identity as an exile:

> There in Mexico, I feel a foreigner and indeed I am a foreigner. But the sensation of feeling abroad in the home country is unbearable.[117]

On the other, it was also due to love. In December 1988, Gelman met Mara La Madrid, an Argentine psychoanalyst and daughter of the poet and lyricist of tangos, Juan Carlos La Madrid. They met for the first time at an Argenmex (Argentines and Mexicans) party. The crush was mutual and immediate. A few months later, Gelman moved to Mexico where she lived and worked. Eventually, Mara became the second and last wife of the poet. Love once again defined important situations in the biography of Gelman:

> The question is not why I do not live in Argentina but why live in Mexico. And the answer is very simple: because I'm in love with my wife, that's all.[118]

From this moment, the presence of Mara would become central to the poet's work, which mentions her on many occasions. In *Valer la pena* (*Worth the Sorrow*), Gelman's twenty-fifth book of poems, to cite one example, three of the titles of this volume recall her: "La conversación con Mara anoche" ("Last Night Conversation with Mara"), "La conversación con Mara esta noche" ("The Conversation with Mara Tonight") and "Te digo, Mara" ("I Tell You, Mara").

No Unexile After Exile

Traces of exile remain, even after exile. In the books that Gelman wrote after his return, first in Argentina and then in Mexico, the painful memories of exile could not be circumvented; they remained as indelible marks on his work.

We will approach three books of Gelman's poetry where all these postexilic features appear more marked and decisive: *Incompletamente* (*Incompletely*), *De atrásalante en su porfía* (*From BackToForth in his Determination*), and *El emperrado corazón amora* (*The Stubborn Heart Still Loves*).

Incompletamente, the twenty-fourth collection of poems written by Gelman between 1993 and 1995, is one of the books where the poet clearly understood that the consequences and disvalues of his exile would remain in force forever in his life and literary work, even after his exile.

He understood that it didn't matter how much time had passed after his return, there were no chances that these traces of exile in his writing would disappear. Therefore, the process of unexile was not going to happen. The consequences of exile would still be read in his work; they became a part of his style, marking his poetry.

It was impossible to turn back the clock or unwalk the walked path. There was no possibility of completeness after exiling fragmentation. That is why Gelman chose as the title of this book the word *Incompletamente*. There was no consolation for what had happened; there was only acceptance . . . incompletely.

In *De atrásalante en su porfía*, his twenty-eighth book of poems, torments and traces of the consequences of the exile also appear, although this book was written between 2007 and 2009. What was staged on this occasion was another devaluation involving exile: the limitation of language. Gelman understood that the possibilities offered in the dictionary were not sufficient to reflect his new perceptions of the world. Therefore, he populated this new work with neologisms to try to shape his new perspectives on reality; in this case, transforming nouns into verbs: Thus flowers "dían"[119] (day), the soul and spirit "diablan"[120] (devil), and lovers try to "lunar"[121] (moon). But it was not only nouns that appeared to alter their grammar. Verbs also took a *Gelman*-way in their forms. It was the language which had to adapt to poetic feel and experimentation, not vice versa. Words needed to adapt to a new emotional authenticity. Thus, the verb *estar* (to be) revolutionizes ("Si estáramos naciente,"[122] instead of "si estuviéramos"), and the verb *venir* (to come) regularizes its conjugation ("lo que vinió,"[123] instead of "lo que vino").

Unable to name things of his new world with the words included in the dictionary ("la lengua no alcanza/ a decir su trabajo"[124]) (language is not enough / to say its work), a new procedure was designed: the strategy of negation. Therefore, beings and things in the world appear in the work of Gelman in a negative form. There is a name but also a "no-nombre"[125] (no-name). The procedure, abundant in the series, refers to the existential digressions of his previous book, *Mundar* (*To World*), where—per Gelman—nothingness and unreason are a fundamental part of the mystery of life. Gelman then mentions the eagle and the "no/ águila"[126] (no/ eagle), no one and "nonadie"[127] (nonobody) and the eternal and always rejuvenated Shakespearean question: to be or "no ser en ser"[128] (not to be in being).

El emperrado corazón amora, his twenty-ninth book of poems written in 2011, follows the experimentations of earlier books. The title came from a poem found in *Cólera buey*, written in 1971:

> Celebrating its machine / the stubborn heart still loves / as if it wouldn't be hit in transverse direction / from back to forth in his determination.[129]

This quote served as an introduction to the poet's new repertoire of stress and concerns. The words as a theme were widely poetized in this new proposal and are shown as insufficient, expressionless, and demure, retained tools lacking the necessary expressive potential. Gelman's textual games, creations, and neologisms accuse this lack of lexical flexibility.

Amorar, for example, a word created by Gelman—as is *atrásalante*, which combined two words into one, *atrás* (back) and *adelante* (forth)—come from the noun *amor* (love) but appear conjugated as a verb. *Amorar* is a necessary word in Gelman's poetic universe and was a word not included in any Spanish dictionary. Gelman was saying that language has its limitations and the available words are not enough to express what the poet feels. That was why it was necessary to invent new words, new expressive possibilities.

There are at least seven poems in this collection that underline this concern: "Dobles" ("Doubles"), "A saber" ("Namely"), "Fugas"

("Leaks"), "Y qué se llama así" ("And What Is So Called"), "Exclusiones" ("Exclusions"), "Divergencias" ("Divergences") and "El jilguero" ("The Goldfinch"). In all of these poems, words appear as if linked with double meaning, exclusive and divergent from the reality experienced by the poetic speaker:

> The word has no hospitals / that heal its world[130]

If the word was not flexible enough to incorporate a reality experienced within a poetic environment in permanent change, as this new proposal suggests, the risk of falling into a frustrating and inexpressive territory was possible. This situation had at least two undesirable derivations: wanting to say what you cannot say or saying what you don't want to say. Combinations could vary, but they always deviated in an expressive dissatisfaction:

> What does it say what we write?
>
> this is an unsheltered question[131]

Paradoxically, what happened on the linguistic level also happened in politics. Or rather, what happened on the political and personal levels was translated to the plane of language. Amid death of comrades and relatives killed, the poet did not find completeness, counsel, or comfort with the available words.

Frustration manifests also in the expressive territory: no joy, no satisfaction, neither fellowship nor brotherhood. The only thing that persisted and remained was a blatant poverty: "La lengua es pobre,"[132] ("Language is poor"), he said in "Fugas." Shortage, loneliness, and helplessness constitute the landscape of this new collection of poems. Perhaps that is why the word *intemperie* (exposed to the elements) was a substantial component of the poetic universe of Gelman, because this term reflected the helplessness, not only political, social, and ideological, but also linguistic.

However, against all odds, the poet's heart was obstinate ("*se emperra*"). It persists, recovers its vital energy, and returns to the fray. Despite so much death, there is a vocation of hope. Despite the pain and hatred, love resurges ("el emperrado corazón amora"). The landscape of optimism flourishes again. A timid clarity among such dark night can be seen, perhaps because nothing makes the night darker than a memory of a glaring bright day. Therefore, the light tells us that darkness exists; love tells us that hate is out there; and life reveals death.

> from the disaster, we got a disaster
>
> and it becomes a hummingbird.[133]

The disaster isn't erased; it doesn't disappear; it isn't forgotten; it doesn't go away; it isn't denied. The disaster remains there until the last day. What occasionally happens—the poet seems to understand—is that from so much death, comes life (the hummingbird), and from much hate, comes love.

The Fallen Compañeros

Gelman's life abounds in terrible and fateful moments, like the murder of his son; the disappearance of his daughter-in-law; the stealing of his granddaughter just a few days after her birth, along with hundreds of fellow countrymen tortured and killed. Gelman knew firsthand the consequences of tragedy and human misery.

In exile with all these calamities in his head, the theme of Death began to appear with greater intensity in his poetic production. This emerging concern is remarkably present in the following five of his books of exile: *Si dulcemente*, *Hacia el sur*, *La junta luz*, *Ni el flaco perdón de Dios* (*Not Even the Forgiveness of God Is Enough*), and *Valer la pena*.

Si dulcemente is Gelman's fourteenth book of poems and the sixth written in exile. Published in 1980, it clearly illustrates this concern about the absence of loved ones, to the extent of functioning as a type of historical-poetic story where countless current events could be read.

Given the fact that news blackouts affected the Argentinian citizens during the years of dictatorship, Gelman's texts reveal data completely unknown at that time to the clear majority of his fellow citizens. Facing the stiff censorship that prevailed in the press and on the radio when reporting the discovery of corpses, Gelman's texts include details of the genocidal operation through the use of metaphors.

In the poem "Quietos por fin"[134] ("Finally Still"), Gelman alluded to one of the secretive operations designed by the dictators, consisting of throwing drugged and undefended illegal prisoners into the ocean or into the middle of the River Plate: "las olas/ del que se tiró al mar" (waves/ of the one who was thrown into the sea) or "sábanas de agua" (sheets of water).

> finally still/all alone/without kisses/the
> compañeros
> they think about me night by night/go around
> sleepless/uncomfortable in sheets
> of mud or water where they are going away/[135]

Among other strategies to humanize those missing, Gelman avoided showing the fallen comrades in a mystified or heroic way:

> they were not gods but men and women that/ needed . . . to make children in the middle of the physical night and in the other night / they were not perfect, by no means / most of them ignore / laws of dialectical materialism / they had not read / *Capital* / they stuttered in economics/[136]

Gelman graphically accentuated that these men and women were common people, not distinguished from the rest. He represented them with their needs, their sorrows, their weaknesses: "necesitaban comer pan/orinar/ vivir"[137] (they needed to eat bread/pee/live).

In a final and disturbing movement, Gelman would close the series with two poems having the same title: "Esperan" ("They Hope"). The title refers to the fallen compañeros who hoped and trusted that their struggle had not been in vain. Gelman stubbornly reaffirmed—through reiterated invocations— the idea of a second chance that provided them another opportunity to complete the work begun in those years:

> they hope we start again[138]

> the poor who will be victorious one day . . .
> the poor who one day will succeed.[139]

Hacia el sur presents a different strategy when dealing with the subject of the fallen comrades. The poem titled "Aquí"[140] ("Here") that can be considered a good starting point for analyzing the new proposal. "Aquí" creates the possibility of imagining a new space where the struggles that were fought during the old time are revisited. The poem presents two distinct scenarios: The first one is negative. There, you encounter several references to the deaths of his colleagues. The other open scenario is positive. Gelman highlighted the brave morale of the popular fighters. The scenario that appears first is defeat:

> here they killed black diana wet of April/
> here her hobbling blue hurt walked by/
> here the miracles of her soul fell as pieces

The positive scenario that precedes the negative seems to rescue from oblivion and prejudgment an unequal struggle, which many colleagues believed in and for which they gave their lives.

> . . . haroldo said yes to each willow /
> and paco said yes to each fight/
> and luis said yes to tenderness/
> and miguel angel said yes to the madness of the angel
> of miguel/
> and jote said yes to beauty/
> and black diana said yes/

"Aquí" represents the precise textual moment where these two realities intersected: The cruel, barbaric, and brutal but sobering reality of the fallen, and the reality that says yes to "dreams," "tenderness," "madness," and "beauty." This space enclosed in the word "Aquí" represents, therefore, the specific location of death as well as the place of love.

The emotional homeland, the homeland that stirs up feelings, the one that is insistently marked by repetition with the adverb of place, "aquí," is unchangeable. This is despite the author's location, despite his countless journeys, despite his exile that forced him to move from one place to the other. Gelman feels as if he is "aquí" in the South, even when he is exiled in the Northern Hemisphere.

In contrast, in the poem "Otras partes"[141] ("Other Parts") the exile and the experience of defeat were overwhelming. Beginning with a title that moves readers away from the South, where the harsh reality lived along with miracles and altruism, "Otras partes" represents the unknown place, where reside the things that feel intimately alien.

> you heard/ my heart? /we're leaving
> with this defeat to someplace else/
> with this animal to someplace else/
> the deceased to another place/

La junta luz, written in Paris in 1982, is dedicated "A las Madres de Plaza de Mayo" (To the Mothers of Plaza de Mayo). This is a dramatic piece that alludes to the worst years of the repression through various accounts. As its name indicates, one of the main actors is the military force. In opposition to their brutality appear the Mothers of Plaza de Mayo, their disappeared children and grandchildren and the Argentine people in their totality.

The military people who are in the scenario on the opposite end of the mothers are verbally abused with derogatory terms such as: "ignorant beasts," "squaddie," "executioner," "torturer," and "dictator." Gelman emphasizes the immorality of the torturers whenever he can. In one case, he shows how a military officer asks for money from one of the mothers in exchange for information or a sign from her disappeared son that would prove he is alive.

> military officer 1:
> 20 million and I'll give you information . . .
> military officer 1:
> 20 million and I'll bring you something, a paper, a sign . . . [142]

Despite the theatrical nature of the work, with its specific directions and notes, Gelman is able to conserve the lyrical nature of his past works in the drama.

The crudeness of the excerpts are taken from reality. Many of the dialogues, as stated in Gelman's footnotes, were gathered from the book *Todos somos subversivos* (*We Are All Subversives*) by Carlos Gabetta, a reporter and ex-director of the Latin American version of *Le Monde diplomatique.* In the following excerpt, while sticking to the historical facts, Gelman emphasized the procedures implemented by military officers against victims of kidnapping and torture:

girl (candice):
a car / two men/
they blindfold me/
in the city/ I know it's the city/
the day/ the daytime/
the underground/
the ladder/
the room/
where is your family? /
the electric prod/
my breasts/
my vagina/
where is your family?/
kerosene in my eyes/
my mouth/
my nose/
naked I'm/[143]

In the context of Gelman's complete literary works, this new book is opposed to *Fábulas*, because of its historical character. Fábulas populates its pages with innumerable mentions of international historical figures, while in *La junta luz* the poetic subject is the Argentine dictatorship. Gelman clearly stated elements and events that alluded directly to the terrible reality of those years in Argentina.

In 1997, Gelman and Mara La Madrid jointly published *Ni el flaco perdón de Dios* (*Not Even the Forgiveness of God is Enough*). This book consisted of testimony from the children of the disappeared prisoners, as well as public figures, artists, and other personalities who were supporting the fight for human rights. The interviewer's questions don't appear in the series, so that the text can preserve the rawness and clarity of the testimonies. This allows readers to immerse themselves completely into the stories with no mediation or distraction from the interviewers.

The new proposal seems to work with the hypothesis of two tragedies: a personal and a collective tragedy. The aim of the work is to show that what happened had reached an enormous number of people. For this reason, a large number of interviewees are included. The intention is to show that each testimony is personal, unique, and non-transferable, because the pain and suffering of every victim is unique, personal, and unrepeatable. This work reveals a perfectly orchestrated plan that was always denied by officials and leaders of the dictatorship. It portrays a perfect scheme of repeated arrests, along with the profile of victims of persecution and torture methods that were used by civil servants and dictators.

The originality of the work and narrative effectiveness result from the way the authors combine different testimonies: those of the recovered children and those of the parents of the kidnapped. Together, they reconstruct a sense of the identity that had been taken from them, an individuality that had been denied and robbed.

The work raises a double question. On the one hand, the identity of the missing parent is reconstructed through children who learn of their parents through photos, memories, reports, and anecdotes from grandparents, friends, and colleagues of their parents. At the same time, the identities of the recovered children are also reconstructed. Throughout the story of their parents, they learn of their origins, their own family identity.

Valer la pena, which was published in 2001 and takes its title from Francisco "Paco" Urondo's poem entitled "Cada día que pasa" ("Each Day that Passes"), goes in a similar direction, trying to keep the memories of horror alive. In this way, this collection of poems remembers and reiterates the names of their deceased friends in several contexts. Remembering and discussing the past is an essential strategy for keeping memories of the victims and suffering alive. Second, it revisits the words of the deceased on their ethics and dreams, so that there is no rushed judgment of them: "los compañeros que/ murieron y esperan/ un mundo sin desprecio" (the comrades that/ died and are waiting for/ a world without disdain.) Accepting the mistakes made during the '70s, this new lyrical composition intended to explain their struggles, justify their life, and move them away from the stereotype and the nonchalance of those who judge lightly: "cuido/ que no se caigan del amor" (I make sure that/ they don't plunge from love).

With this book, Gelman tops off a long journey of sharing his poetry in more than ten countries. The permanent enunciation of the fratricidal genocide in his poetry functions as a spell against the darkness of past years. Spreading the word serves to bring awareness. Gelman corrected Theodor Adorno's idea that "writing poetry after Auschwitz was barbaric"[144] by saying it would be barbarous not to write a poem giving an account of the horrors that took place in Argentina.

"The Child Was Born"

While in exile in Rome, Gelman began a search for his disappeared son and daughter, Marcelo Ariel and Nora Eva, and his daughter-in-law who was seven months pregnant at the time.

In 1978, two years after their kidnappings, Gelman learns through the secretary of the Vatican that his daughter-in-law María Claudia gave birth before she died. He doesn't know if it's a boy or a girl because the message only read: "the child was born."

In the following interview, Gelman gives details of his search:

> I know that the child was born. Because Claudia was due in less than a month, and that set in motion many forces in Europe: among them the Vatican. The news came from a Jesuit priest, Father Cavalli, who worked for the Secretary of State, in Italy. The priest told Gelman that he received the news from Buenos Aires in February of '78.[145]

According to witnesses, the Gelman family was last seen in the *Centro de Detención Automotores Orletti* (Clandestine Detention Center Automotores Orletti) in Buenos Aires. Because that was a usual destination for Uruguayans being persecuted by the Argentine dictatorship, Gelman extended his search to Uruguay. It is unknown why

María Claudia relocated to Uruguay. What is certain is that all the clues of her and her son or daughter's whereabouts pointed to Uruguay.

Jorge Elías in his book *Maten al cartero: posdata del asedio a la prensa durante las dictaduras militares del Cono Sur* (*Kill the Mailman: Postscript to the Siege of the Press During the Military Dictatorship of the Southern Cone*) refers to the collaboration of Argentine and Uruguayan governments being fundamental to the framework of the Condor Plan.[146] The police and military forces of the Southern Cone worked together to prevent entry of activists and suspicious people into their countries.

Robert Hill, American ambassador to Argentina, understood the link between repression systems on both sides of Rio de la Plata:

> Our evaluation of the information we have has convinced us that the kidnappings of Uruguayan refugees in July and September were done by Uruguayan and Argentine forces acting secretly and together.[147]

Public Campaign to Recover His Granddaughter

Trying to find his unknown grandchild, Gelman published an open letter in the weekly newspaper *Brecha* of Montevideo, on April 12, 1995. The letter was addressed to his grandson or granddaughter who would have been nineteen years old and probably lived in Montevideo without knowing her or his identity: "You may have been born in October of 1976 in a concentration camp." The letter serves as his formal introduction. Gelman talks about himself and his search for Marcelo Ariel and his daughter-in-law, Claudia. He tells the story of Marcelo Ariel's murder and aspects of the life of Claudia and her pregnancy: "She must have given birth under supervision of a doctor who was an accomplice to the Argentine dictatorship."

In the later section of the letter, Gelman centered the story on his granddaughter or grandson. He said that he or she was probably relocated and illegally given up for adoption to a member of the repressive forces. He also talked about a strange double parental circumstance: "It seems strange to me to talk to you about my children who were your parents that you never met." Gelman then showed contradictory feelings toward her current familial situation:

> On the one hand, it disgusts me that you call "dad" a military officer or policeman or murderer of your parents. On the other hand, I always wanted for you to be loved, raised well, and educated with whatever family you stayed with. However, I never stopped thinking that, even so, there had to be some flaw in the love they had for you, not because they are not your biological parents—how it is said—but because consciously they must be aware of your history and they took control of it and they falsified it. I imagine that they have told you many lies.[148]

When Gelman imagines possibly meeting her, he asks himself what he would do and how he would proceed in this hypothetical situation:

> All these years I have thought about what to do if I found you: whether to pull you out of your home or to speak with your adoptive parents and reach an agreement that would allow me to see you and spend time with you, always on the basis that you would know who you are and where you come from.[149]

He also considered the age his grandson or granddaughter must be and asked himself if she would be mature enough to be able to handle the situation with all the sadness, anguish, and pain it brings:

> It worries me that you might be too young to know what happened. To understand that those parents that you love and that you think are your parents are not really your parents. It worried me that you would suffer a double blow, an axe blow of fate to the weaving of your identity in formation.[150]

The doubts and fears in the letter that Gelman wrote to his granddaughter would widen. Gelman began to imagine a possible meeting, an early resolution in the case of the disappearance of his granddaughter. At the end of the letter, Gelman foresaw a tough decision to be made about identity:

> But now you're grown. You can know who you are and decide what to do with who you were. There are the Grandmothers of

> Plaza de Mayo and with a DNA test we would be able to know with scientific precision the origin of the disappeared children. Your origin . . . [151]

Finally, the letter recalls the excitement and affection that her expecting parents felt for her:

> They dreamt about you and about a world that would be good enough for you. I would love to tell you of them while you tell me about you. To see in you my son and for you to see him in me: We are both his orphans. To repair in some way the pain that the military dictatorship caused our family. To give you your story of which you have been deprived. You are grown.[152]

Doubt assails and troubles him again at the end of the letter:

> Maybe you have the green eyes of my son or the brown eyes of your mother, that were so bright, tender and devilish. Who knows how you might be if you are a boy or a girl. Maybe you can uncover that mystery to then uncover another one: That of a meeting with a grandfather that awaits you.[153]

The letter did not bring progress to the investigation, as was expected. Gelman grew tired of his protests being ignored, and he intensified his press campaign in the Argentine and foreign papers. In 1999, Gelman brought to light a new series of open letters addressed to the commander-in-chief of the Argentine Armed Forces, Lieutenant General Martín Balza, and General Eduardo Cabanillas. The letters explicitly incriminated Cabanillas, who served as second chief in the Automotores Orletti concentration camp at the time of the disappearance of his children. Gelman gives accurate dates of when the general oversaw the secret center:

> During that time, on the 24th of August 1976, my son Marcelo Ariel, 20, and his wife María Claudia García Irureta Goyena de Gelman, 19, were kidnapped from their home by Orletti personnel and taken to the concentration camp.[154]

Much of what Gelman knew was attributed to the accounts of retired military officers made on November 17, 1977. Three times he demanded that Balza investigate the actions of his subordinate:

> Are you going to do something? Perhaps General Cabanillas did not know what Captain Cabanillas knew? And what are you going to do in that respect, mister Lieutenant General Martín Balza? It would not cost you much to consult the lawsuit I mentioned: 4 1 70035/1 located in the judicial archives of the Superior Council of Armed Forces, folder 10720, record 80739. It is on you that the six bodies of the lawsuit don't disappear. Also, the duty of reading them: concerning your immediate subordinate, commander in the armed forces.[155]

Finally, he bids farewell with the certainty that "the pain needs words" to be soothed and truth needs justice to avoid repetition:

> Speak, mister lieutenant general! It would be easier for you to figure out the destination of María Claudia and her baby. You have access to those files. If you do not do it, then you will need a cure for insomnia because a conscience that does not allow sleep can only be calmed by death.[156]

One of the first achievements of this campaign was the identification of General Eduardo Cabanillas, one of the five most powerful active generals in Argentina who also took part in the murders. It also exposed various Uruguayan presidents who went along with the dictatorship.

On April 1, 2011, the ex-general Eduardo Cabanillas was sentenced to life in prison. On the same day, Gelman published his open letter to General Balza and sent a series of open letters to the ex-president of Uruguay, Julio María Sanguinetti, who refused to investigate the case.

Gelman gave details of his and his wife Mara La Madrid's investigation in an interview with Horacio Verbitsky in Madrid.

> Every night we analyzed the signs to see which ones were false. We counted on the help of Uruguayan survivors. Mara read thousands of documents and books. I had difficulty

> remembering what I read. I think it is a limitation linked to my close relationship with the victim, my own family. Mara did it as a citizen and because she loved me.[157]

In another stretch of the interview, Gelman praised the success of the public campaign and immense support received from friends and strangers from more than forty countries who wanted to help the cause:

> What was most important in finding my granddaughter was the press campaign and all the people who helped. More than a hundred thousand signatures, gathered from forty countries, of writers, authors, painters, and ordinary people. Letters of contribution came from Saramago, Chico Buarque, and many others. The letter from Günter Grass to Julio María Sanguinetti caused him to lose the *honorary doctorate* he was waiting on from a German university. This accomplished what we hoped for: A neighbor, who saw a baby being brought to a house with no children, associated this with the open letters that we published. This caused a shake-up in Uruguay.[158]

Gelman mentioned that among those who joined his campaign was Nobel Prize in Literature winner José Saramago. In 1999, Saramago sent a public letter to President Julio María Sanguinetti, demanding the cooperation of the Uruguayan government in Gelman's investigation. The letter began with the Nobel Prize winner of 1998 introducing himself:

> My name is José Saramago, I am a Portuguese author and I currently live in an island of the archipelago of the Canarias. . . . Do not find it strange that culturally and socially, Latin America matters to me. . . . I am a Nobel Prize in Literature winner, but I'm not writing from that position. I don't even think it is because I write books that I am writing to the President of Uruguay.[159]

Saramago directed his letter "man to man." He immediately explained Gelman's case and demanded answers: "Where is she?" He then suggests an exchange of roles between president and poet:

> The President of the Oriental Republic of Uruguay is not named Juan Gelman, but if he was . . . What would he do? If Juan Gelman, let's pretend, was the President of Uruguay, surely Dr. Sanguinetti would knock on his door and say: "Help me find my grandchild." And I'm sure Juan Gelman would use his power for the service of justice.[160]

At the end, he emphasized the need for a quick response:

> Help Juan Gelman, help justice, help the deceased, those that were tortured and those that were kidnapped. That would help the living that cry and search for them. Help yourself, help your conscience, help your disappeared grandson that you do not have, but may have.[161]

The end of the letter was honest and precise: "I have nothing else to ask you because I've asked for everything, mister President."[162] Afterward, the president of Uruguay received numerous letters from writers and artists around the globe, including Chico Buarque, Fito Páez, Eric Hobsbawm, and a collection of Mexican authors supporting the demand.

"We Are Both His Orphans"

After a long and intense investigation, thanks to the work of human rights associations, Gelman discovered that María Claudia was transported to Uruguay on an Argentine Air Force flight after spending two months in detention at Automotores Orletti.

Once in Uruguay, she was imprisoned in the Service of Information and Defense center (SID) in the capital of Uruguay. On November 1, 1976, in the military hospital, she gave birth to a girl, whom she nursed only for a few days. They were quickly separated. In a prophetic way, Gelman foresees the event in his open letter of 1995.

> She must have given birth alone, under the supervision of a doctor that worked with the military dictatorship. They took you from there and relocated you—that's how it almost always

> was—to an infertile couple with a husband that was affiliated with the police, or military, or a reporter that was friends with either. At the time, there was a dreaded waiting list at the concentration camp: The names written down hoped for a child that was stolen from the female prisoners, and with few exceptions, they were murdered after giving birth.[163]

Thanks to the investigation by Uruguayan newspaper *La República*, Gelman determined that days after giving birth, María Claudia was transported to a secret army center, known as "Base Valparaiso," where functioned a fleet of taxis driven by agents who spied on the movements of the population. The latest news confirmed that Captain Ricardo José Medina Blanco, alias "el conejo" (the rabbit), removed María Claudia from that center. His mission was to kill her.

The participation of Medina was revealed by the Uruguayan ex-president Jorge Battle to the leader of the *Frente Amplio*[164] (Broad Front), Zelmar Michelini. However, as a consequence of the disgraceful *Ley de Caducidad* (Amnesty Law) that prevailed in Uruguay, this crime and hundreds of crimes committed by the Uruguayan repressors were never prosecuted.

The newborn girl was taken to a Uruguayan police family by Medina. Shortly after, she was registered with the name María Macarena. Journalist Ana Laura Pérez interviewed Gelman and he stressed the need to know the truth:

> The search for the remains may sound like a necrophilic act, but it has to do with something else: Each one of the 30 thousand people—as you know the mass number of people wipes away the individual stories—each existed, lived, and was a person with their own story. Finding a place to rest is an old habit of our humanity since the beginning. It is bringing them back to their story and, in general, to the history of our civilization.[165]

Twenty-four years after her birth, Gelman's granddaughter was finally recovered and her identity was reestablished. Her "appropriator father," ex-commissioner of police, died when they uncovered the crimes of wrongful appropriation and false adoption. Journalist Horacio Verbitsky published the latest details of the investigation in *Página/12*.

> And what we wanted happened. A female neighbor obtained my phone number, called me, and said: This happened next door to me. We compared the dates and the information fits. Only the DNA was missing. We went to Uruguay discreetly and covered the secret meeting with my granddaughter with a tribute they were doing for me.[166]

After Gelman's relatives contacted her, Macarena submitted her DNA tests to confirm her identity. In 2004, she legally assumed the surnames Gelman García and began the process to gain Argentine citizenship in addition to the Uruguayan that was given by birth. After recovering his granddaughter alive, the poet urged the Uruguayan and Argentine governments to identify the destination of his daughter-in-law, as well as to give details on her kidnapping and disappearance.

The Granddaughter Recovered in Gelman's Poetry

The disappearances of his daughter-in-law, granddaughter, colleagues, author friends, and children were present in not just one, but all Gelman's books of poems written in exile. They are inherent themes in Gelman's poetry; they are urgent realities of his biography. Like Octavio Paz once said: "The biography of a poet is in his work."[167]

The investigation and recovery of his granddaughter, who was missing for almost twenty-four years, left an impression on his work that is permanent and one of the biggest marks of his poetry. These circumstances are reflected in the following five books: *Citas*, *Carta abierta*, *La junta luz*, *Valer la pena,* and *Mundar*.

Citas, the second poetry book that Gelman wrote in 1979, reflected all of these years of fruitless searching and uncertainty. At first, these poems manifest a tension between what he wants and the painful reality of being far from the homeland and without the affection of his family. This homesickness is shown to be elusive and clashes with his failure to recover his stolen granddaughter: "*gasto la vida/ en morirme de vos*" (I spend my life/ in dying of you).

The gap between what he wants ("you," his granddaughter) and the sad reality of absence (the time that passes without her) manifests itself in an unavoidable absence that goes in three different directions: since neither "I" have "you" nor "you" have "me," and neither of "us" have "them." Therefore "we are both their orphans," because "my son and daughter-in-law, your parents" are still missing.

However, on a formal level in a second poetic moment, this fissure between want and reality would dissolve. The repeated use of "you" attached to a noun or a verb produces the illusion of an effacement of the borders between "I" and "you." It is to say that there is an intermediate instance between the "I" who looks and an absent "you" that does not manifest. In one of the poems of this collection, Gelman writes, "duermo de vos"[168] (I sleep of you). The verb in first person (I sleep) joined with the pronoun in second person (you) would give the impression of a confusing indivisible unit. It is difficult, therefore, to discern who the voice that speaks is.

The strategy is an oscillation that occasionally insinuates a separation between the "I" and the "you"; while in other cases, these pronouns allude to a shared situation, that is, the "I" and the "you" appear juxtaposed. The examples are eloquent:

> ... *dulce mirar de vos*[169] (. . . sweet glance of you)
>
> ... *dolor de vos*[170] (. . . pain of you)
>
> ... *sombra de vos*[171] (. . . shadow of you)
>
> ... *consolación de vos*[172] (. . . consolation of you)
>
> ... *pena de vos*[173] (. . . sorrow of you)
>
> ... *noche de vos*[174] (. . . night of you)

As can be seen from these excerpts, the confusion between the limits of the pronouns "I" and "you" is not resolved. On the contrary, it is exacerbated. It is as if the poet was saying the missing beloved are not absent, they live in me: "*como esposos que no se puedan ya/ apartar/ secreta unión en el centro/ muy interior del alma*"[175] ("as spouses that already can't/ move aside/ secret union in the inner/ soul"). Perhaps the impossibility of being with his granddaughter and loved ones has its counterpart in his poetry. Since in it, everyone *desaparecido* emerges as a unit through diverse literary recreations.

> child very along with my child/
> skin in skin/ medulla that burns me
> in a unique flame where youme.[176]

As a final synthesis of this unity, Gelman needed to create a new word. At the end of the verse he writes "vosmí" (youme), a union between two pronouns *you* and *me*.

In a more direct way, a second level emerges with endless images and resources that reflect many years of search, pain, and uncertainty. The granddaughter appears, for example, allegorically represented as an "*árbol regado/ con la sangre del admirable amor*" (tree watered/ with the blood of admirable love). The love in this case is represented by her parents, the children of the poet, who have been kidnapped and assassinated. Even so, they continue watering and illuminating the growth of their daughter.

In *Carta abierta*, written in 1979, Gelman offered a curious symmetry between his missing son and his absent granddaughter. Most of these poems are dedicated in memory of Marcelo Ariel, as was already clear from the epigraph. However, at times the choice of the poems' addressee seems to fade away. In this way, the poetic voice begins to talk to a very young child, with dozens of diminutives that appear to come together in a dialogue with his granddaughter:

> little water of your way to look at[177]
>
> what little bits can I already put together?[178]
>
> do you fly outside of me little soul?[179]
>
> little face that usually/ enlightens up the brute in me?[180]

> little soul/ as happiness in the hand[181]
>
> the little face you were[182]
>
> do you carry death / with your little hands[183]
>
> your little vein broken and shattered?[184]

Two final quotes illustrate Gelman's poetic attitude in this first stage. On the one hand, as Rainer Maria Rilke said, "What is beautiful is no more than/ the beginning of something terrible, that we can scarcely bear."[185] The horror is derived from the loss of a loved one and not from anything less important. The second quote, corresponding to a prologue that Julio Cortázar wrote for a work of Gelman's, highlighted one of the greatest virtues of the author of *Gotán*:

> Gelman's work will give ample evidence of poetry superimposed on the state of terror, turning that which is negative into a creative force. . . . a man who was cut off from his family, who has seen his dearest friends die or disappear. . . . no one has been able to kill in him the willingness to undertake this amount of horror as a positive counterblow, creator of a new life.[186]

Cortázar later illustrates one of the strategies most used by Gelman, referring specifically to the resemantization of some terms:

> When Juan turns the noun *dictator* into a verb, the first reaction in the quick reading is of surprise and almost of scandal. One sees the verse as if it were ruined by a printing error and suddenly, it gives the jump (when it's given, it's what one hopes) and one discovers the richness of this metaphor so deeply linked with our reality in which everything is "*dictadurado*" (dictatorshipped), in which the notion of going on or lasting ("durar") becomes unbearably manifested. They will continue "*dictadurándonos*" (dictatorshipping us) while we don't learn and apply the

infinite counter language of the word and of the revolution. And this is not more than an instance in the continuous denial of what is accepted and what is acceptable that gives Juan Gelman's poetry its capacity for maximum transmission. Hence the masculine becomes feminine and vice versa to trample on the canons of stereotyped thinking. Without hesitation, many words that we handle passively become active and functioning. The poem ceases to be a communication to contact oneself. Juan and his reader cease to be alone and they separately follow the path seeking to lead us toward ourselves.

La junta luz, the seventeenth of Gelman's books of poems published in 1982, dedicated "A las Madres de Plaza de Mayo" (To the Mothers of Plaza de Mayo), is constructed following the model of a dramatic oratory in verse. It is divided into seven sections, structured as if they were a theatrical play. At times choral, with musical rhythm in others that are marked by the chants of protestors that demand justice, the work is reminiscent of a form of prayer or of response, with sentences dedicated to the deceased and missing.

The voices that are represented in this work are: the "mothers" of Plaza Mayo, the "military" that personify the genocidal military, the "little boy," the "son," and the "little girl" that are the voices of the missing. On a more personal level, the voices of his own children and granddaughter are represented, along with the "chorus" that functions as the voice of the people of Argentina, and various combinations such as "mother-chorus" and "mother-tree."

The new piece developed in four main stages and includes the orchestra, mothers, chorus, and the Pirámide de Mayo (Pyramid of Plaza de Mayo).

The action begins with a mom of Plaza Mayo who forcefully, simply, and precisely notes the absence of her son, marking the beginning of the drama.

Mother:
So, he is no longer here.[187]

From this opening begins the drama of absence. What follows is a tragedy as stopped in time. The mothers, the children, and the torturers appear to be accompanied by a chorus that moves between, repeating in poetical tone what the mother ("mother-chorus") says and supporting the claim of the missing detainees.

Among the most important lyrical moments of the work are the endless torture sessions suffered by the abducted child. Although he tirelessly repeats his infant reality, "*Soy un niño*"[188] ("I am a child"), the phrase is not powerful enough to stop the horror:

> military man:
> State your first and last name, your war nickname,
> which group you belong to, the zone where you serve
>
> child:
> I am a child.
>
> military man: (gesture to hit)
> Now you will confess that you are a guerrilla
>
> child:
> Yes. Now I am a guerrilla
>
> military man:
> Didn't you see that you're a guerrilla? Why didn't you
> say anything before?
>
> child:
> I said it because you hit me so that I would say it
>
> military man: (gesture to hit)
> I didn't hit you so that you would tell me that. Say that I
> wouldn't hit you so you would tell me that.
>
> child:
> You didn't hit me for me to say that.

military man:
You see? That is to say that I wouldn't hit you if you said that you were a guerrilla. That is to say, you are a guerrilla

child:
I am a child

This text perfectly illustrates the climate of the era. The little boys and girls who scream and protest are the children who look for their absent parents and their identities.

Another of the surprising aspects of the text is the inclusion of quotes from Gelman's other poetry books. The following verse, for example, refers exactly to the end of the poem "VII" of *Carta abierta*.

Voice (in off. Singing / tenor):
Where are you at/ saddest by lukewarm?[189]

The "loans" continue, for example, when the mother asks the same that Gelman asked years before when *Carta abierta* was published.

do you uncontrollably fly for your comfort?[190]

do the shadows greatly sweeten your death?[191]

do you speak through the walls of your pain?[192]

do you burn the night of your torturer? Don't you?[193]

You wouldn't want to sleep/ but dreaming/[194]

The dialogue that Gelman maintains with his previous poems mixes with the feminine voices of these mothers. He also cites fragments of *Notas* ("talmente llovío sangre/ sangre llovió por mi país") (it literally rained blood/ blood rained for my country) that tucked in the circumstances of the kidnapping of his granddaughter and death of his son, mixing with his voice and the feminine voices of these mothers. His masculine voice assumes his role as Father of Plaza de Mayo. Therefore, this cross inserts the continuation of the search: "¿hasta cuando?...hasta encontrarte"[195] (until when?...until I find you).

> all of a sudden / an enormous silence / they are all
> frozen in gesture /
> a banner lowers and covers the left half of the stage—
> one hears the sound of the ropes when it goes down—it
> says, "until when?" another banner lowers and covers
> the right half of the stage. It says, "until I find you"[196]

Valer la pena, Gelman's twenty-fifth book of poems, constitutes a certain global vision of all the wanderings that took place politically and poetically in his previous works: his militancy and the social commitment, the repression and the abduction of his children, his exile and banishment, but above all, the search for his granddaughter Macarena. The book brings together 136 poems composed between the years 1996 and 2000. The first year coincided with the moment when he began to go to certain data on the whereabouts of his granddaughter, after a long investigation; the last was when he finally found her.

The theme of the political assassinations, as well as elements of his own biography and the biography of his son ("Tumbas cavadas en el agua") (Graves dug into the water) need to be enunciated and denounced. This willpower, textually explicit, was destined to retrieve the memory of his children and granddaughter, kidnapped in the Clandestine Detention Center Automotores Orletti.

> Clandestine Detention Center Automotores Orletti
>
> Who draws the hands of the night
> with the vacuum they don't have? Is

it possible to turn the tongue over, to feel
its hole of nevers? To see it
as if it weren't before?
And that, and after that and later how?
And how much blood is that?
Grab all the words, stomp on them
to bring them to another light, to another mouth.
To make them fly in dispossession.
To make them to begin again.[197]

Mundar, his twenty-seventh book of poems, published in 2007, crowned the desperate search for his granddaughter that turned out to be directly mentioned. The new proposal doesn't seem to have either a new or a unique concern. There are questions and themes present in his previous books, such as the memory of the fallen comrades, especially when he mentions Paco Urondo in "Paco." One can also find the following themes: (1) the subject of love as a final goal ("…es amor/la cuchara… amor/los jinetes… amor/la palabra… amor/y amor"[198]) (…is love/the ladle… love/the horsemen… love/the word… love/and love); (2) the subject of the mysterious poetry, always present in his visions ("La diosa Palabra… solo visita a los que ama"[199]) (The goddesses Word… only visits those who she loves); and (3) the nostalgia for the old good times at the *milonga* with his young friends from Villa Crespo, present in "Pisadas" ("Footprints"), "Malena," "Volver" ("Return"), and "Baires."

The theme of the missing granddaughter takes on a textually important presence, especially in two compositions titled, "El pasado vuelve" ("The Past Returns") and "Nos veremos" ("We'll See").

In an interview with Silvia Friera for *Página/12*, Gelman would confirm the thematic variety of the new book. Along with the intimacy of the text, diverse resources express anguish and desolation: sharp caesura cuts in poetry that speak for the interruptions and separations of loved ones, nouns that turn into adjectives, and irregular verbs that are made regular. Catalan poet and essayist Joaquim Marco highlighted it in an article that appeared in the Spanish newspaper *El Mundo* in 2014.

> From "Hechos," the poet will make use of the sharp cut-short-pause and will go even further in "Descubrimientos"

> (Discoveries). . . . The words are understood as "matter" and in consequence, can alter their form: "averaver" (to see to see) for example; the nouns turn into adjectives: "huelen a leche madre" (they smell of mother's milk); also changes in the accents, such as in "páis" (country), and the language, even becomes intimate in "Andrea escribe a Marcela" ("Andrea writes to Marcela"). The poetic formulas resort to baroque mechanisms, such as the paronomasia [play on words]: "recuerda/ cuerda" ("memory/ rope").[200]

After years of meticulous and desperate search, Gelman succeeded in finding his granddaughter Macarena. However, many other questions and searches would remain unanswered and abandoned.

Gelman, a Committed Journalist

Journalism was another of Gelman's great passions until his final days. Added to his love for poetry and his strong political convictions, the three passions coexisted like good neighbors, in harmony and without conflict. Gelman consistently dismissed possible conflicts between these apparently very distinct spaces:

> It so happens that journalism is simply a neighbor that lives on a different floor of poetry. And although I do not believe that journalism has helped me as a poet, its practice has permitted me to get in contact with diverse realities. They are distinct languages, intimately, deeply rooted with different mysteries of life. While poetry reveals the secrets of words and of existence, journalism brings what is hidden to the public, the secrets of power.[201]

Technically, Juan Gelman's journalistic career began early in 1950, when he sporadically collaborated with the internal magazine of an insurance company called *El Asegurador*. However, beyond the corporate data, journalistic activity for Gelman would be closely linked to his political convictions.

His first experiences in political publications date to late 1954, with his collaborations in *Nuestra Palabra* and in other weekly papers associated with the Argentine Communist Party, such as *Orientación* and *La Hora.* He would later act as a correspondent for *Xinhu,* a news agency of the People's Republic of China government.

Gelman would recall one of his first contributions, in the mid-1950s, in an interview that appeared in *La Maga*: "I moved closer to the core of a magazine that was called *Muchachos* where there were writers like Damato and Cronda and the poet David Álvarez Morgade."

In 1958, Gelman edited the magazine *Nueva Expresión* with sociologist Juan Carlos Portantiero and writers Andrés Rivera and Roberto Hozni. The publication, which addressed the current cultural and social relevance of the country, sought to redefine the literary critic from a left-wing perspective.

His intense career as a journalist continued in 1966 as a book reviewer for the magazine *Confirmado.* Three years later, he served as editor in *Primera Plana,* a glossy political, cultural, and current affairs weekly magazine, published between 1962 and 1973, and *Los Libros*, a monthly magazine that assessed publishing activity in Argentina, with reviews of the country's publications and authors. At *Panorama*, a weekly magazine of general interests with a new emphasis on politics, he served as press secretary and worked with Homero Alsina Thevenet, Miguel Grinberg, Daniel Muchnik, Carlos Ulanovsky, Francisco Urondo, Horacio Salas, and Edgardo Da Mommio, who became the cultural supplement editor of the daily newspaper *El Mundo.*

Between 1971 and 1973, Gelman held the office of editor in chief and director of cultural supplements for the daily magazine *La Opinión*, guided and funded by Jacobo Timerman. Collaborating with him were Tomás Eloy Martínez, Francisco Urondo, José María Pasquini Durán, Osvaldo Soriano, Rodolfo Walsh, Horacio Verbitsky, Miguel Bonasso, Nicolás Casullo, and Hermenegildo Sábat, among others. Gelman remembered an anecdote that illustrates what it was like to work for for *La Opinión* during those years:

> Once something very funny happened. Soriano was preparing a special edition about science fiction literature in Argentina. The pages had to go on Friday nights because the supplement was printed on Saturday and was distributed on Sunday. And here comes Hermenegildo Sábat, who was the graphic designer of the supplement, worried because

> he was missing about forty lines to complete the page, and Soriano had already left. I sat down and wrote a little story called "The Mission": a few Indians who, supposedly, are in Spain to see someone, who supposedly is the Brave Warrior (Cid Campeador), with a lot of chained prisoners, walking along the banks of the river. The Indians look and say, "No, these are barbarians. It's better that we return." I published it signed by an author from Santiago del Estero. (And that Timerman would forgive me, but Soriano took this money on behalf of his fellow countryman and we all went out to eat at *El pulpo*.) The funny thing is that years later, an older friend of Soriano, who devoted himself to studies and archives of science fiction, found Osvaldo in exile and asked him: "Dude, what happened to that writer from Santiago del Estero that once appeared in *La Opinión?*" Soriano, dying of laughter, told him: "No, that was Gelman. He had to fill a gap and wrote something." The man, in an extraordinary rage, went to his archive, which he managed to save with great effort, and he pulled out the tab for the writer from Santiago del Estero and ripped it, while furiously complaining to me "You don't take this seriously!"[202]

In 1973, Gelman joined *Crisis* magazine as writing secretary and held this position until 1975. The magazine, funded by patron Federico Vogelius, soon became a transcendent magazine locally and internationally, reaching a circulation of fifty thousand. Very few journals reached this circulation during this era. Among other collaborations, he emphasized the contributions of Eduardo Galeano, Mario Benedetti, Vicente Zito Lema, and Aníbal Ford. Due to Triple A's constant threats, Gelman quit in mid-1975 after working on twenty consecutive volumes.

In 1974, he also worked as head writer of the daily newspaper *Noticias*. The publication responded to the political line of Montoneros. He worked with Francisco Urondo, Horacio Verbitsky, Rodolfo Walsh, and Miguel Bonasso, the director of the newspaper. Gelman remembered how he worked during those years:

> . . . with a gun in the desk drawer. . . . our offices backed up

> to the Costume Museum building, where the wife of Lorenzo Miguel, the right wing union leader, was named director. Opposite we had an office of the Juventud Sindical (Peronist Youth Union.) We were luxuriously surrounded.[203] When they put the bomb in *Crisis,* the police inspectors saw the rubbish and said that it had been a work of art. They made a double play. If we limited our journalistic work and didn't take any provision, Triple A came and flew into the building or shot up the cars that had the print's materials. If we took defensive precautions, the police came and we were processed for carrying firearms.[204]

That year, Gelman also participated in *Perú: el poder al pueblo (Peru: Power to the People)*, where he wrote a burning prologue, calling on the militants to collaborate with a revolutionary project against the oppressive Peruvian situation of the 1970s. He worked with Carlos Delgado; Carlos Franco; Jorge Fernández Maldonado; Juan Velasco Alvardo, the ex-president of Peru; and others. The volume was published in Buenos Aires in *Los cuadernos de Crisis*, number ten.

After his exile in April of 1975, and especially after the military coup, Gelman's journalistic works would significantly dwindle, like that of most committed journalists during this time of censorship. In 1979, with the triumph of the Nicaraguan Revolution, Gelman began to collaborate with *Nueva Nicaragua*, the emerging news agency from Managua. In 1987, with the arrival of democracy in Argentina, Gelman started working from day one at *Página/12*, although he was still in Paris waiting for a favorable judicial resolution.

These first articles, written in Paris, appeared to address a unique but multifaceted theme, as defined by Horacio Verbitsky: "Crimes committed by an organized unit of power against defenseless human beings." The series of articles included extensive notes on Klaus Barbie's trial, the Nazi leader known as the "Butcher of Lyon," who served as chief of the Gestapo in the French city.

As Gelman mentioned in his articles, Barbie was accused of numerous heinous crimes, as well as being responsible for the disappearance of several militants of the French Resistance, the capture of Che Guevara in Bolivia, and the coup d'état of the Andean country that ousted the first female president in the history of Bolivia, Lidia Gueiler Tejeda. According to Verbitsky, during these nearly three decades writing for *Página/12*,

Gelman also focused on "The Shoah, the Palestinian massacres in Israel, Bush and Obama's wars in Afghanistan and Iraq, the unforgiveable dictatorships in Africa, Asia, and in Latin America." The style of his articles avoids the use of turning words into adjectives. It focuses on data analysis and offering concrete facts with the aim of allowing them to speak for themselves.

He returned to the country in 1988 and was incorporated as the editor of *Página/12,* where he began directing the cultural supplement.

According to Mara La Madrid, during this period Gelman began to show interest in Mexico's political and social situations. His interest became stronger with the uprising of Zapatistas. His most well-known interview was with the ex-deputy commander of the army, Subcomandante Marcos, as Gelman's wife recalled:

> Beginning in 1994, he was interested in the Zapatistas. He even traveled to Chiapas. My daughter Marcela let him borrow a very small, yellow sleeping bag. I bought him a pink jacket that was waterproof, thermal and light. And a canteen. When we said goodbye, we realized that we had forgotten to give him the compass. Anyway, he returned despite torrential rain at that meeting. I still encounter people who say how Juan furiously complained about the lack of chivalry of some men. Although I do not know exactly, it seemed like he went to sleep in the rain to allow women and children to sleep inside.[205]

In 1997, Gelman collected his articles and published them in Buenos Aires with the title *Prosa de prensa* (*Press Prose*) under the label Ediciones B. Two years later, the second volume, entitled *Nueva prosa de prensa* (*New Press Prose*), appeared from Ediciones Grupo Zeta and Editorial Vergara of Buenos Aires. Journalist Rogelio García Lupo, Gelman's friend, highlights the impact of these articles on national mass media:

> This collection of articles is actually a great essay about our time, administered with a dropper for those who do not have time to read more than newspapers. Gelman accomplished the feat of the writer of the press of any era, grabbed the reader's attention with attractive titles, making them submerge in the

text, making them think.[206]

After 2001, with the attack on the Twin Towers in New York City and the monumental political, social, and economic crises in Argentina, his researches would focus on the war against terrorism, the concentration of wealth, climate change, and every topic that was directly or indirectly related to his definitions of unfairness and inequality. Verbitsky remembered those years of investigation and obsession:

> In 2001, he started writing about Iraq, Afghanistan, gringos, the CIA, and Al Qaeda. From there he started criticizing neoliberalism, globalization, and the destructive force of what he called the "Imperio empantanado" ("Bogged-Down Empire") which became an obsession for him. As results of those investigations, in 2003 Gelman published *Afganistan/Iraq: el imperio empantanado* (*Afghanistan/Iraq: The Bogged-Down Empire*).[207]

Art, literature, and politics would always be constant concerns in Gelman's life and work. In 2005, he published a collection of articles called *Miradas* (*Looks*). The book included short biographies and analyses of poets, writers, musicians, painters, actors, and scientists such as Marcel Proust, Paul Valéry, Henry Miller, Franz Baermann Steiner, F. Scott Fitzgerald, George Grosz, William Burroughs, and others.

The essays attempted to link the life stories with the development of the art produced by these artists. The portraits focused on unknown aspects of the protagonists, far from popular or traditional stereotypes. One of the pieces reviews the life and work of Ezra Pound, who, according to Gelman, could address the propaganda for Mussolini by writing "the most wonderful poem against usury." In another piece, Gelman said that Flaubert " . . . thought every dogma was spiritually fake, whether it is religion, progress, Catholicism, or democracy." The idea was always the same: stay away from stereotypes and portray a creative personality under a humanistic and universal light.

In 2005, Gelman began to collaborate with a very popular newspaper from Mexico, *Milenio,* and with the Cuban news agency *Prensa Latina* until his last days. In 2008, many of his essays had also been published in the monthly publication *Cuadernos Hispanoamericanos* of Madrid.

The following year, two new compilations of Gelman's articles appeared with the titles *Escritos urgentes I* and *Escritos urgentes II* (*Urgent Writings I* and *Urgent Writings II*). They were published by the editorial Capital Intelectual of Buenos Aires and explored contemporary reality. As their titles indicate, these were issues that demanded immediate attention, including fratricidal wars, new and complex political phenomena taking place in Latin America, sustainable economy, the problem of food shortages, and underdevelopment.

According to Mara La Madrid, Gelman had very strict work ethics. His work was never late:

> When we travel, his notes were prepared in advance. Sometimes he would send everything all together to the newspaper, or if we were in Tepoztlan on the day it had to be sent, he looked for a public fax to do so.[208]

In his final days, he used the computer skillfully. He learned to take advantage of the Internet:

> He had access to international newspapers and other sites, which he investigated. He printed everything in color. A new ink cartridge had to be bought all the time. Every time, he searched for information that could be of interest for the readers. When he found something of interest, he made a script. This took him a day, a day and a half. And then he wrote the article.[209]

Days before dying, according to La Madrid, Gelman showed his shaking hands and said:

> "I don't know what I'll do to write tomorrow's article."
> "Juan," I told him, "everything can't be done."
> Then he asked:
>
> "What will I live on?"
> I almost killed him.[210]

Gelman will be remembered by many generations of journalists and in many different places. During the last part of his life, he lost hope, but continued to be cordial and affectionate in intimacy. A few days before his death, the Spanish newspaper *El País* published a farewell note:

> He used to walk, smoke, and read. He maintained a critical support for the government of his country. Until only a few months ago, he wrote a weekly column in the Argentinian paper *Página/12*. He was supportive of his soccer team (even from afar). It was Atlanta, from the second Argentina division.[211]

He supported protest movements, including Occupy Wall Street, the Spanish 15-M movement, and the Mexican Yo Soy 132, although he felt politically hopeless because of the immense power of the globe's richest 1 percent and the multinational corporate forces that overpower the political system. "A system to quell the spirit had been installed," he concluded in one of his final interviews.

Poetry, a Beautiful Lady

Juan Gelman's poetic calling began when he was very young. By the age of eight, he had become an avid reader of poems. At only eleven years old, he published his first verses in the magazine *Rojo y Negro*. According to what he said later, it cost him quite a bit to get published: "A lot of times I tried to bribe them by sending fifty, sixty stamps, but they rejected them. Until they finally published me."[212] The first published poem said: "Fue un sueño muy hermoso para ser cierto, señor; el destino poderoso, envidioso, lo rompió."[213] (It was a too-beautiful dream to be true, sir; powerful fate, envious, broke it.)

Joseph Gelman, a passionate reader of history and political books, influenced Gelman's love for poetry, which lasted a lifetime. His brother Boris, who used to read Russian poems in their original language, was also a great inspiration for him. "Poetry was like hypnosis to me; the sounds attracted me on one side and the mystery of the inapprehensible words on another. . . . "[214]

In 1948, he began studying chemistry at the Universidad de Buenos Aires but left several years later to dedicate himself to poetry: "There was a day where I declared myself a poet. I abandoned then the School of Chemistry. Also, I was in love and left everything. I began working as a truck driver, transporting furniture. I sold auto parts, and through the bills I used to issue to my customers I discovered the pen, the ink and the typewriter."[215]

When one asked Gelman why he wrote poetry, and didn't write short stories or novels, he responded with humor: "I'm sure that I write poetry out of pure laziness, because the advantage of verses is brevity. The poem is short, the lines are shorter."[216]

In 1955, at only twenty-five years old, he founded the legendary literary group, *El Pan Duro*:

> It was 1955 with machine-gunned people hoisting sailors up on their shoulders in Barrio Norte, with humiliated multitudes and the revenge of the minorities celebrated in galas and embassy receptions. It is also the birth year of *El Pan Duro*.[217]

With his friends from the Communist Party, Gelman created a literary group to self-publish, distribute, and promote their poetry books. Members of the group were Héctor Negro, José Santirso, Jorge De Luca, Atilio Jorge Castelpoggi, Alberto Wainer, Hugo Ditaranto, Rosario A. Mase, Julio César Silvain, Nicolás Reches, John Hierba (Samuel Nemirosky), Carlos Somigliana, José Luis Mangieri (who edited many of the books), Alvarez Morgade, Luis Alberto Navalesi, and Guillermo B. Harispe. Juana Bignozzi joined them later.

The system created by this group distributed their books and materials through the sale of tickets in advance that could be redeemed for copies of published books. They also organized public readings in libraries and neighborhood clubs. During one of their activities in the theatre La máscara, the group met Raúl González Tuñón, who was a quite respected poet by intellectuals of the time.

According to the chronicles, on that night, La Máscara was full of people drinking gin and discussing diverse topics such as the writer's commitment to art, consequences of the Spanish Civil War, the recent death of Dylan Thomas, and conflict between the Church and Peronism. The chronicler heard the following conversation between Rosario Mase and José Portogalo, who, in addition to being a great poet, was also a port worker: "Look, Mase, I'm the enemy of the sonnet. I like Quevedo, who is eternal. But you, however, reconcile me with the sonnet because it's full of stuff."[218]

Luis Alberto Navalesi (who shares an anthology with Gelman) passionately talked about philosophy with students, who listened carefully. He went over the duties and obligations of the writer's art. Héctor Negro was enthusiastic about local soccer. He commented on results of the last matches and explained that the first poets who influenced him were the tangos as well as Darío, Almafuerte, and Miguel Hernández. At the end of the evening, ". . . when dawn commanded [all] to leave and lower their voices, some want to pay, but the waiter stopped them: 'Everything is paid, good night, gentlemen' and points to where sat a small man, a great man, an elf: Raúl González Tuñón."[219]

Gelman appreciated Tuñón and respected his work. He was one of Gelman's greatest teachers. "Raúl González Tuñón taught me finesse. An extraordinary finesse," Gelman said in an interview in *Revista Veintitrés* in 2001. "He lived modestly with his job as an art critic on the newspaper *Clarín*. And I never saw him in a resentful attitude. He was passionate. When the USSR-China break occured, he was with China, just because Mao wrote poetry while Khrushchev was the son of millers."[220]

The first book that the group *El Pan Duro* decided to publish was *Violín y otras cuestiones* by Juan Gelman. The group that defined itself as "Militants of poetry, with similar ethics and aesthetics," decided it with a solid unanimous vote. It was published in 1956, under the imprint of Manuel Gleizer, who thirty years earlier had published the first books of Raúl González Tuñón, Macedonio Fernández, and Jorge Luis Borges. Tuñón wrote the prologue of Gelman's first book. One of the paragraphs of the preface reads:

> In this singular "*Violín*" and in the *Otras cuestiones,* healthy winds of civil assertiveness float in those torn poems. Gelman's poetry does not respond to this or that rigid perspective, but to the perspective of a citizen of the world. The shape of his poetry is agile, fresh, varied in tones and hues. Its prevalent form is free verse, and it is logical, because it corresponds to the foundation of our identity.[221]

In an interview by Carlos Santos Sáez and Adrián Rimondino that appeared in the magazine *Lea,* Gelman expressed his admiration for Tuñón:

> I admire González Tuñón, for his poetry, in the first place, and also for his vital attitude. He was a free man, very

generous with the young ones who approached him. He radiated an influence that not only came through his books, but also through his personality.

After this first publication and before the encouraging results, the group decided to publish *Bandoneón de papel* (*Bandoneon Made of Paper*) by Héctor Negro in 1957 and *El tiempo es un barrio* (*Time is a Neighborhood*) by Julio César Silvain and Héctor Negro in 1958.

In 1963 the best works published in *El pan duro* were published in an anthology. The compilation reflected the spirit of the group. The anthology included poems by Gelman, Luis Alberto Navalesi, Hugo Ditaranto, Guillermo B. Harispe, Rosario A. Mase, Alberto Wainer, Julio César Silvain, and Héctor Negro.

The same year, with the ban of the Communist and Peronist parties, Juan Gelman, Luis, Alberto Navalesi, José Pastafiglia, and Lázaro Kanonchi were arrested because of their active participation in strikes and political rallies.

Poetry and political activism were always integral parts of Gelman's most intimate identity. By the end of his life, he had published almost thirty books, and never abandoned his convictions or militant commitment.

Poetry and the Power of a Spent Match

Gelman's poetry discusses many topics, such as politics, human rights, injustice, and freedom. His poems express his fears and obsessions, loneliness and exile, defeat, death, and hope. Among these themes, a topic remained invariable from his first works until the end of his career. This is the persistent question of the nature of poetry. His work was filled with issues relating to the essence of his work, his reason to be, his principles and identity: What is poetry, Gelman asks himself; how do you conquer it; what are its science and its secret?

In the following pages, we will address the way these issues are reflected in six books by Gelman. We will specifically address: *Gotán, Mundar, Violín y otras cuestiones, Velorio del solo* (*The Alone's Wake*), *Cólera buey*, and *Valer la pena.*

In his first book, *Violín y otras cuestiones*, published in 1956, the exercise of poetry is inevitably manifested like an essential and sometimes painful work: "me duele el aire, sufro el sustantivo"[222] (air hurts me, I suffer the noun). Poetry requires awakening and an attentive soul; it molds expression and words, regardless of clocks or dictionaries:

> who told me to fight with grammar,
> curse me at night, fiercely
> screeching, deny myself, complain,
> moan, cry[223]

Poetry appeared unexpectedly in a tenacious and stubborn way, as an overwhelming force that assaulted his nights, whether he was in Paris, Managua, or Medellin. It was not a work that could be postponed. Poetry was born not of reason, but from tireless obsession. Interviewed by Enzia Verduchi, Gelman tried explaining this in *Brecha*:

> As Pavese said, one traces a graphic where the obsession is very high and the expression is on zero. As you achieve the expression, the obsession gets wasted, the line descends, bringing up the expression. There is a point where they cross each other and the poems are written more happily.[224]

As observed in the following stanza, Gelman feels "condemned" to live with that mysterious force.

> . . . who sent me walking pregnant with phrases,
> wear an imaginary hat, go
> to wait for a rhyme in the corner
> like a punctual and unhappy boyfriend[225]

"La poesía es una manera de vivir"[226] (Poetry is a form of living) concludes Gelman in one of his first poems.

In "Poema" ("Poem") from *Velorio del solo*, Gelman's third poetry book published in 1961, the mysterious force of poetry is presented under the form of a "poetic ardor." Poetry recurrently and insistently emerges. It is furtive assault and passion:

> Like love, like love you insist,
> nothing can get you away,
> not even the hardest rock that I throw against me.
> You come, hit, light foot,
> like love you climb,
> pure bliss,
> surf of the dark unknown wonder[227]

Poetry is ungraspable and indescribable, but it is also a precise tool. In the last section of this book, poetry is considered as a privileged vehicle to present the reality of the soul. In "Foto"[228] ("Photo"), a short and apparently simple poem, Gelman compared poetry and photography. The conclusion is astonishing; the photographic portrait results in a pale and inefficient copy of reality when compared to poetry's force of suggestion. The photographic representation appears as a stereotypical caricature of a much more complex reality. The elusive materiality of reality can only be captured by poetry with fairness and accuracy.

> Photo
> In the photograph your eyes turn sweet
> there is your face from a side, your mouth, your hair,
> but when we are excited by love
> under the surface of the night and the clamor of the city
> your face is forever an unknown land
> and that photography is oblivion, another thing.

Photography is "otra cosa" (another thing) the poet says, something far from the reality of love, that which excites "under the surface of the night and the clamor of the city." While photography can only represent reality through a simple plane on a limited surface, poetry presents endless variants and expressive possibilities to represent a complex and ever-elusive reality.

In "Preguntas,"[229] from the first version of *Cólera buey,* published in 1965, the poem appears as an untamed force that interrogates the author. It questions, reveals, and explains. It is offered as the reason for his passion, like a homeland finding answers against the beasts of oblivion.

Questions

since you travel through my blood and know my limits
and
awaken me in the middle of the day to lay myself in
your memories
and you are the fury of my patience tell me what the
hell I do
why do I need you who are you mute alone traveling
along
the reason of my passion why do I want to fill you
completely of me
and encompass you finish you mix myself in your little
bones and you are the only homeland against the beasts
of oblivion.

In an interview by Enzia Verduchi for *Brecha*, Gelman was asked about the circumstances around poetry's creation: "I think that everything that is written is a failure as an attempt to capture poetry. Poems can be written, but writing poetry is another thing . . . If one insists on this burning job that is poetry, it's because one awaits a miracle, but like Dylan Thomas said, the miracle of miracles is that sometimes they occur."

Lastly, in *Valer la pena* (2001) there is a fun crosslinking with his wife, Mara La Madrid, that delivers more hints about poetry's priority in Gelman's daily life. Curiously, the domestic reality is presented in contrast with the existential reality of the poem. "La llave del gas" ("The Gas Tap") and "Nota al pie de 'La llave del gas'" ("Footnote to 'The Gas Tap'") are two good examples of this procedure:

The Gas Tap[230]

The wife of the poet is
condemned to read or listen to the
smoking verses that the poet
just took out of his soul. And more:
the wife of the poet
is condemned to the poet
who never knows where
the gas tap is and pretends
questioning to know
when he only cares to ask
about what has no answer.

The "realidad de la cocina" (reality of the kitchen) and the "realidad de la poesía" (reality of poetry) are presented as two unconnected spaces that require coexistence. In the first, things are "open and closed," without giving rise to more extensive options; however, the poetic universe is governed by the world of "precipice," by an infinite universe of possibilities where perception, intuition, chance, mystery, and desire play an unknown but important role.

Footnote to "The Gas Tap"[231]

The wife of the poet was angry
with the poem "La llave del gas."
She doesn't see why the target word of the word,
or the ambiguity of the word,
or the wounds that the words produce,
can stop anyone
from knowing where the gas tap is and
how it opens and closes. She is right.
The poet is wrong because
the key of the word, let's say, doesn't close,

nor open, and even pretends that it doesn't exist,
and even less its target word, that hurts with its
ambiguity or its emptiness.
The reality of the kitchen reassures,
there are taps that close, open and work
accomplishing the function of demonstrating
that they are things that close and open,
and sound in my head since yesterday
that I cannot close.

In October 28, 2005, while receiving in Salamanca the XIV Queen Sofía Award of Ibero-American Poetry, Gelman confesses in his speech that poetry is "un tirar contra la muerte" (a permanent struggle against death) and a way to understand life. At this point in the road, Gelman says, poetry must discover mysteries yet incomprehensible, must "esperar un milagro" (wait for a miracle), name the occult, the human tragedy, and escape the "principio de realidad" (principle of reality) because poetry is dreams and desire.

In 2017, after nearly fifty years of conscientiously poetic work, questions related to the origin of poetry remain unanswered in Gelman's work. In *Mundar*, his twenty-seventh book of poetry, Gelman understands the inability to define what is indefinable. Poetry has no name, no law to govern it; it is autonomous and untamed.

What is Known?

Of poetry, nothing. It comes, trembles
and tries to light a spent match.
Can you see something? Nothing.[232]

The nature of poetry is unknown. Poetry is powerful and can do everything, even light a spent match, but at the same time, it is nothing. It is an ungovernable and unclassifiable force:

Poetry is not a bird.
And it is.
It is not a feather, the air, my shirt,
no, none of that. And all of that.
Yes[233]

School of Resentment

Gelman thought that the science in poems cannot be explained or reduced to a determined and specific school of thought. When he was asked about certain interpretations of his work by specialized critics, Gelman respond with humor: "A couple of years ago, in a place of La Mancha whose name I don't remember, they sat me next to six European professors skilled in what I write. And every one read his work on the subject. And there I learned many things."

At this point, Gelman appears to agree with the "School of Resentment" theory developed by American professor Harold Bloom, who argued that reducing the creative force of an artistic piece to a predetermined theoretical framework reduces its expressive strength and limits its aesthetic autonomy.

No matter the school of analysis—New Historicism, structuralism, Marxism, or postcolonialism—any discipline of contrasting analysis will tend to sweep away the libertarian essence of any artistic work if it proposes a univocal reading. On this subject, Bloom and Gelman agree.

In *Eso*, his eighteenth book of poems, Gelman is critical of those "teachers of poetry" who seek to interpret "our existence on earth" as "mere suffering."

the professors of poetry/
they laid it upon the table/
stabbing little knives here/there
picking out little bone or flesh/they

passed it through various lights/
sociological/historical/Xs

they inspected the generational
tissues/finding
famous ancestors/little mystic fingers in an intestine
fine/or[234]

Gelman sought to avoid reductionism in order to prevent biased readings. He posits that the meaning of Shakespeare's poetry, for example, should not be limited to sociological interpretations of the time during which it was written. Gelman believed that, despite efforts to define and classify the meaning of an artistic work, poetry follows its libertarian and unclassifiable ways. The multiplicity of poetic meaning will then remain mysterious and elusive. The interpretations of critics are by no means definite.

. . . while on the subject/poetry/
as straight as the way of the sword
beneath the zinc sky /
unstuck itself/peeled the layers from itself/honored
itself/started walking . . . [235]

Christian Mysticism

Exiled thousands of miles from his hometown without institutional support and with hundreds of family members and colleagues murdered or missing, Gelman became interested in second-century BCE mystic poetry. It was a deeply religious poetry that inspired and transported him to centuries past, when the soul and heavenly deities sought communion in harmony.

What probably drew Gelman to the mystic poets was their privileged relationship with the Supreme. Most mystic poets were brimming with a collection of practices, discourses, traditions, texts, and experiences that sought transformation of the human spirit. Perhaps Gelman wrote this type of poetry to ward off the homesickness that he felt and to mitigate the remoteness of his location. We shouldn't forget that it was a moment of great insight. Gelman sought refuge in religious mysticism to rethink his work, assuage the concerns of exile, and find peace and quiet during death and desolation. The writings and testimonies of mystic poets probably moved Gelman, who carried the shadow of a terrible recent past that he would be forced to recollect every day of his life.

Three fundamental characteristics of mystic poetry are also seen in the work of Geman: asceticism (which seeks to lead a life sheltered from earthly temptations, open only to reflection), contemplation (which, in turn, was important for achieving the purification of the soul), and acceptance of the limitations of intelligence. Since the intellect is incapable of understanding God, it is only the heart that can "understand" and discover divine truths.

At least three collections of Gelman's poetry reference this Christian mysticism: *Comentarios*, *Citas*, and *Incompletamente*.

Comentarios, Gelman's tenth book of poems and the first that dabbles in the ways of mysticism, was written between 1978 and 1979. It is composed of sixty-four "commentaries" that establish dialogue with past texts written by various personalities of deep religious faith. In this contrast between mystic texts and his own poetry, Gelman mentions Hadewijch of Antwerp (who ascribed to the movement of the thirteenth-century Beguines); Saint Teresa of Ávila (1515–1582), who is especially prominent in Gelman's book *Citas;* Saint John of the Cross (1542–1591); Saint Ignatius of Loyola (1491–1556); Luis of Granada (1504–1588); and Fray Luis de León (1527–1591). The selection also includes prophets such as Zephaniah (belonging to the group of the minor prophets of the Old Testament) and apostles including Saint Paul (Saul of Tarsus, known as the apostle to the Gentiles).

Using many of their experiences as a source of poetic inspiration, Gelman opens a channel to talk about his own life in exile.

In the first verse of "Comentario III (santa teresa),"[236] for example, Gelman seems to clearly refer to ascetic confinement and the isolated environment that fosters mystic doctrine:

> . . . everything
> . . . silent or walled in . . .
> and no one
> would do anything other than close.

Both Saint Teresa of Ávila and Saint John of the Cross insist, through their mystic texts, that the highest achievement of the soul is not in ecstasy or the mystic experience itself, but in total obedience to conformity of the human will to the divine will. The words of Gelman could well be translated as numbness and temporary suspension of ego and reason, so that the spirit is freed from the dictatorship of sameness and can find its own way to embody these mystic precepts. Maybe that's why Gelman suggests that among the things that must remain isolated is his own self: "ni siquiera/ yo entre"[237] (not even/ myself enter).

Another convergence seen in this book is between medieval mysticism and the tango of the River Plate region. Gelman felt the need to connect the mystic, medieval reality and the reality of present-day Argentina. He bridged them with the existential experience of tango. Tango, along with mystic poetry, created an excuse for him to refer to Argentina and the reality of exile. He references tango composers such as Homero Manzi, José María Contursi, Cátulo Castillo, Homero Expósito, Carlos Gardel, Alfredo Le Pera, Roberto Firpo, and several others.

The process of redefining tango poetry occurred through a type of collage where Gelman mixed the concerns and anxieties of his exile with fragments of old tango lyrics, as one can see in "Mi Buenos Aires querido" ("My Beloved Buenos Aires"), "Anclao en París" ("Stuck in Paris"), "Volvió una noche" ("Returned One Night"), and "El día que me quieras" ("The Day You Love Me"), among other poems.

Rescuing the "local urban forefront," Gelman frequently used expressions that allowed him to display a prominent oral tradition though the use of the mystic existentialism of tango. Lunfardo terms such as *amuro, chamuyo,* and words with a double tilde, such as *sangrándomé* (I'm bleeding myself), *soñándomé* (I'm dreaming about me), and *olvidándomé* (I'm forgetting me) attempt to reproduce the orality Gelman gradually was losing from being thousands of miles away from his homeland. As expressed in an interview, "The tango has this view of exile. All these stories of women leaving men alone, of the pain that causes and of the other sorrows present in the lyrics of tango, are nothing more than symbols or representations of other abandonments."

The other poetry collection that continues the spiritual and mystic writings of *Comentarios* is *Citas*. Also written in 1979, this book, Gelman's eleventh, consists of forty-five "citations" that refer exclusively to texts of Saint Teresa of Ávila, religious founder of the Discalced Carmelites.

The choice of Saint Teresa of Ávila, whose name appears in parentheses next to the title of each of these numbered citations, is not a coincidence. *Citas*, like the texts of Saint Teresa, illustrates the moral conflicts that manifest when one attempts to live a full spiritual life. The point to understand in the case of the Spanish poet is that the only way to reach God is through death.

> How sad it is, my God,
> this life without you!
> Eager to see you,
> I want to die . . . [238]

This distinction that is made between the body and soul is the knot that ties the verses together. For Saint Teresa, the body relates to the material and is practically despised, because it is far from the immateriality of the soul and, therefore, the possibility of being-with-God. Therefore, what is desired is death. In the religious context, it is synonymous with the transcendence of the body:

> Who is the one who fears
> the death of the body,
> if within it one obtains
> an immense pleasure?[239]

In *Citas*, the body-soul separation goes through similar paths. The body is understood as a holder or recipient of pain. Therefore, in many of his compositions, the body is metaphorically associated with fire and burning: ". . . alma que me brillás/ cuerpo que hierve"[240] (. . . soul that shines me/ body that boils).

The distance between desire and reality is unfathomable. That is why mismatched feelings appear, confusing desire with death and the happy memories of loved ones with the great sadness caused by their absences. In "Cita III (santa teresa)" for example, desire ("sentada a la sombra de su deseo"[241]) (sitting in the shade of your desire) and death ("viva muerte que te acompaña ser"[242]) (living death who accompanies your being) appear combined as two impulses in permanent conflict, guiding the dense world of Gelman's exile.

This constant contradiction derived from frustration manifests at the formal level by the exuberant use of neologisms, varied breaks, abundant use of diminutives, and a strange, almost childlike conjugation of the verb inflections: "para que almés mi desasido rostro"[243] (for you to soul my broken face).

If in the texts of Saint Teresa, the interlocutor is always God, *Citas* refers to the situation of exile, focusing on the philosophical idea of soul, spirit, and country. The word *alma* (soul) appears in thirty-four of the forty-five poems in this series. Its presence is overwhelming and strongly suggestive. *Citas*, therefore, is also an exploration of the immortal substance of human beings through the painful and lonely experience of exile.

His homeland is not named, although it is clearly included in the book's dedication ("a mi país") (to my country). In these nearly fifty citations, there is no reference to specific places in Argentina. The curious absence reveals his deepest concern: the impossibility of returning home.

The ever-present God in Saint Teresa of Ávila has its counterpart in Gelman's ever-present Argentina. The feelings of incompleteness and dissatisfaction are present in both collections. There is a primary object of desire that appears evasive. The frustration felt in pain, pain in agony, solitude, and reclusion: both poets are where they do not want to be and obsessively refer to where they want to be. The case of Saint Teresa naming God mirrors the case of Gelman avoiding the mention of his cherished and forbidden home country.

Another book in which the continued mystical theme of exile can be observed is *Incompletamente*. Gelman wrote his twenty-fourth collection of poems in Mexico City between 1993 and 1995. This book provides an intertextual mix with medieval Italian poets, especially Tuscans like Guido Cavalcanti. In one of his poems, Gelman uses the allegory of sueño (slumber) and vigilia (wakefulness) to represent a poetry that is not silent, "que no quiere dormir"[244] (that does not want to sleep), and that fights back against the suffering or "burden" of exile:

> cast the burden-sufferive upward/open
> the dream that does not want to sleep.[245]

As noted in "Preguntas," in Gelman's imagination, poetry appears to be formulated as an alternative to the "sufridera" (burden-sufferive) and as a force against the beasts of oblivion ("contra las bestias del olvido"[246]).

Jewish Mysticism

Five years after writing *Citas* and *Comentarios*, Gelman decided to recompose or rewrite texts primarily from Judeo-Spanish mystic literature. He stated on more than one occasion that this interest arose after reading the texts of the Jewish esoteric school, the Kabbalah, and the Judeo-Spanish, Italian, and German traditions forged by poets of the twelfth, thirteenth, and fourteenth centuries:

> My encounter with the depths of Jewish and Hebrew culture came later, when I became familiar with exile. Then I began to ask myself many things, why we were defeated, about the killings in Argentina, the disappearance of loved ones, the absence of a person from their country, the absence of the country from that person, the language of its people. . . . That feeling led me to read the Kabbalah for the first time. And I found it somewhat in line with what was happening to me: namely, a view of life in exile.[247]

Two books where this intertextual work clearly appears are *Com/posiciones* and *Dibaxu*. Written between 1984 and 1985, *Com/posiciones*, his nineteenth book of poetry, contains references to at least nineteen Judeo-Spanish mystical texts and poets. There are references to the writings of Solomon ibn Gabirol, an Andalusian philosopher and poet born in Malaga; Abba Yose ben Hanin, who lived in Judea during the first century of the classical period; Rabbi Yehuda al-Harizi, translator and Judeo-Spanish poet of the Middle Ages; Eliezer ben Jonon, a fictional poet created by Juan Gelman; Joseph Tsarfati, a poet of Jewish origin and translator of *La Celestina* into Hebrew who died during the Sack of Rome (Sacco di Roma) at the hands of the troops of Charles I on May 6, 1527; Yehuda Halevi, doctor, philosopher, and Judeo-Spanish poet and creator of the "Zion genre," a poetry of exile that refers to the faraway Jerusalem; Samuel ha-Nagid, a Talmudic erudite, grammarian, philosopher, warrior, and Judeo-Spanish poet; Emanuel de Roma, a heretical poet who introduced the sonnet to Hebrew poetry and who was a contemporary of Dante Alighieri; and Rabbi Isaac Luria, founder of the Kabbalistic school of Safed and Jewish mysticism philosopher, among others.

The collection also includes other sources like the Hekhalot—an esoteric Jewish literary genre originating in the Old Age; the Dead Sea Scrolls, a collection of about eight hundred Jewish texts written between 150 BCE and 70 CE whose discovery revolutionized the archeology of the area; and other mystical texts, such as Abū Nuwās's, a classical Arabic poet born in Persia, and Ramprasad's, an eighteenth-century Bengali Hindu poet who was considered a saint.

The chosen geographies are revealing. Gelman recreates his experience of exile by drawing on the writings that occurred in the main cities and towns of the Middle Ages, such as Toledo, Provence, Palestine, Babylon, Jerusalem, Baghdad, Basra, Constantinople, Vicovaro, Tudela, Granada, Córdoba, Alexandria, Fermo, Safed, Kumarhatta, Calcutta, and Comino.

The book opens with an epigraph which, we are told, explains that the intention of this book is not to translate other people's works ("traducir es inhumano"[248]) (translating is inhuman). The intention is to provide an intellectual and poetic exchange where both poets—the referenced and Gelman—share a starting point. In other words, the unity and coexistence between the two texts or what Gelman called *consubstancia* (consubstantial), share a common purpose: the view and situation of exile. We do not have to change anything, says Gelman: "hay que dejar esa belleza intacta y poner otra para acompañarla"[249] (you have to leave that beauty intact and put in another one to accompany it). In this exercise of accompaniment lies the power of this text, transforming pain or "astro frío"[250] (cold star) into the "sol que está por venir"[251] (sun that is to come).

A break is clearly observed in the title of the work. In *Com/posiciones,* the title is cleaved by a back slash that divides it into two new semes: "com" and "posición." One might consider the possibility of taking a "position" regarding the preceding text to review it (compose it) with a new perspective and give it new meaning. Therefore, the title refers to mixing, to intertextual work, to reading and rewriting.

The theme of exile appears as an inescapable constant. It often takes the form of a missing loved one and at other times expresses scorn at the impossibility of return. In the following poem that comes after the original text of Yehuda al-Harizi of the twelfth century, Gelman redefines the concept of exile, expanding its margins and presenting it as being responsible for great plunder. It is not limited to geography or lost affection, but as the poet says, "the deportation of my tongue."

The Expelled

they threw me out of palace/
I did not care/
I was banished from my homeland/
I walked the earth/
they deported me from my tongue/
it accompanied me/
you separated me from you/and
my bones extinguish/
living flames embraces me/
I'm expelled from myself/[252]

This defense of the country's language is essential in order to preserve the traits of his own identity. He felt that this identity was in danger, contaminated by the other languages surrounding him. In this specific moment of Gelman's life, the language was French. In others, it was Italian, English, etc. This concern takes many forms. One of the most symbolic is present in the following poem that "accompanies" the verses of Gelman's fictional poet, Eliezer ben Jonon.

The House

is not in the sea my house/nor in the air/
in the grace of your words I live/

—Eliezer Ben Jonon[253]

The territory of language represents the last frontier. Language defines the way in which we understand the world. "Deport us from it" is one of the most violent acts of dispossession.

Of all the images that abound in this group of poems and that represent his struggle, we choose "Los dos llantos" ("The Two Cries"), because it clearly shows the idea of exile as an irreconcilable departure. In this case, Gelman is inspired by both national realities that Judeo-Spanish poet Samuel ha-Nagid had experienced firsthand.

The Two Cries

your heart hears two cries/
yours/of birth/
the other/if you go/

—Samuel ha-Nagid[254]

Com/posiciones expresses the will of Gelman to venture into the past of the Jewish exile that he had studied in search of new expressive ploys and innovative ways of looking at eternal core themes: exile, the homeland, poetry, and love. In an interview in *Página/12,* published on September 17, 2000, Gelman provided more details about this Jewish vocation: "Surely the Jewish dimension shows in my writing; how denying the candles on Friday or Passover meals has left its mark on me."

Dibaxu, Gelman's twentieth collection of poetry, includes twenty-nine bilingual poems in Sephardic and Castilian. The selection contains an introductory "Scholium" that opens the work. A "coexistence" or dialogue is established between the two languages, sharing a concrete objective that the poet explains in the following way: "As if seeking this Castilian foundation . . . had been my obsession. As if the extreme loneliness of exile compelled me to search for roots in language, deeper and estranged from my language." These are the roots that Gelman finds in the Sephardic language.

With this book, Gelman attempts to locate a "lost innocence," as he says in an interview with Enzia Verduchi, ". . . a tenderness from other times that remains alive and therefore full of comfort." This "innocence" that is recovered through a linguistic journey into the past—"from el Cid" to the Reconquest of the Iberian Peninsula, and thus to the expulsion of hundreds of Jewish families—will allow Gelman to speak of his own exile. Expulsions and linguistic exiles seem to defy temporal differences and establish a dialogue with poetic materials written five hundred years ago.

Through this action Gelman intends to portray his River Plate emotions in Sephardic, a dead language, with the objective of recovering a latent rhythm and tone that he believed lay dormant within it. The Sephardic *avla* (speak) with which Gelman "cowrote" this new book remains strong, beyond the distance of time, beyond the five hundred or six hundred years that separate its production from the present. It is recognized as valid, expressive, and suitable for consumption, "aviarta para bever" ("able to be drunk").

Gelman seems to tell us that time is merely a relative circumstance, a construct of the human mind that presents no obstacle to expressing emotions. Sensitivity—according to the poet—can be expressed in the same way, making use of the same linguistic material. As Gelman says in his text "La casa del amor" ("The House of Love"), presented at the IV Meeting of Latin American Jewish Writers in 2006, "Poetry is infinite" and time is no more than an anecdote through which men and names pass.

It seems that the connection between the remote past, expressed in Sephardic, and the present exile, expressed in Castilian, helps Gelman find shelter, the "comfort" and "innocence" he lost. Only then, through time and language, can Gelman humanize and renew his own syntax, avoiding burnout and withdrawal. This necessary detachment and the loss of familiarity with Sephardic words, as Gelman states in his "Scholium," are great opportunities to open a space of "reflection on language from the most calcined place, poetry" (reflexión sobre el language desde su lugar más calcinado, la poesia). His is a reflection that is born *Dibaxu* (below) the surface of contemporary Castilian, in the Sephardic heart of a burnt-out language.

Moreover, this self-imposed exile from his mother tongue, in search of what Gelman called *el sustrato* (the foundation), opens the possibility of a silent, underground dialogue, possessing the innermost layers of subjectivity. As if he were to learn to speak again, joining words one by one like an illiterate child, Gelman also retrieves the innocence of the simple things in life.

XXIV

loving you is this:
a word that is still to be said /
a small tree without leaves
that makes a shade /[255]

In conclusion, *Dibaxu* seems to incarnate an innovator volition, a new way of looking at the world, from below, from *dibaxu,* from the substrate of the Sephardic syntax, with the objective of opening other perspectives. New perspectives emerged, capable of discovering new things in the old things that had been many times observed. Writing in Ladino allows this new positioning. This is the perfect place to get lost in a distant world and to find and recognize oneself.

leaving from your side
I discover
the new world
from your side /[256]

Gelman's Poetic Sky

The influences in Gelman's poetry are very broad. His references come from diverse provenances and schools. Gelman finds inspiration in the classics, in the Christian medieval mystic poets, in the Sephardic and the Spanish Jewish poets, as well as in contemporary artists. In this catalogue are included social poets, romantics, Latin Americans, tango composers, and existentialists, who coexist without apparent conflict.

That big "sky of poetry," following the image that Gelman cultivates in one of his famous compositions, "Ruiseñores de nuevo" ("Nightingales Again") comprises universal poets like Sappho, Saint Teresa of Ávila, Yahuda al-Harizi, Garcilaso de la Vega, John Keats, Rubén Darío, Stephane Mallarmé, Roque Dalton, Paul Verlaine, Raúl González Tuñón, Walt Whitman, Cátulo Castillo, and many others.

Evidently, successions and influences are raised instead of hierarchies. Gelman proposes a generous canon, an open pattern, where there is a place for everyone: This is a transhistoric, translinguistic, and transgeographical accumulation that becomes capable of synchronizing different periods in the history of art, different languages, and distant geographies. Latin American art merges with art from big European metropolises, thus highlighting the universal character of poetry. There are neither frontiers, nor time, nor space, nor linguistic limitations. The classic poetry that emerges from the earliest centuries mixes with the existentialist poetry of tango. It goes from Christian to Jewish poetry, from the classical to the modern, without interruption.

The list seems chaotic and disorganized but could be much broader if every single poet that Gelman cites in his work was included. However, there is a hidden dictate that reveals an intentionality.

Two points can be kept in mind regarding the many poets who are named in Gelman's work. The first refers to the "theory of influences" from Harold Bloom. The North American critic focused part of his research on the analysis of the influence that literary works exerted on other works. Just as in *The Anxiety of Influence* and his later book, *The Western Doctrine*, the NYU and Yale professor would understand that, in return for influence arises a competition, a dispute, for a place in the history of literature. Naming Whitman, Pavese, or Mallarmé means maintaining a cordial dialogue with them but also engaging in a fight for survival.

According to Bloom, the literary tradition is neither just a horse race nor a friendly process of transmission, where the new text continues the strong preceding text. It is a relentless battle between the previous genius and the one who aspires to be a genius. The reward is literary survival or inclusion in the literary canon. This way, a new metaphor always implies a reference to a previous metaphor. The new poetic image must be original, although part of a precursor image; a renewing point of view must be proposed.

But independent of this fight to enter literary history, there is another critical issue. The literary influences that preceding texts exert define a literary ideology and ethic. In Gelman's case, these define his preferences and his territories—a story and cartography, as he elects his forerunners based on their ethical and ideological quality. Thus, the "big sky of the Gelmanian poetry," that initially seemed chaotic and disorganized, offers a homogeneity that goes beyond political and historical periods, beyond languages and regions.

In that big sky of poetry there is a common element, a pattern that is evident in his book *Hacia el sur*. In many of the poems in this book, the cited poets reveal an ideology and/or aesthetic that Gelman shares and pinpoints. In "*Los poemas de José Galván*" ("José Galván's Poems"), as in "*Los Poemas de Julio Grecco*" ("Julio Grecco's Poems"), "*Ruiseñores de nuevo*," "*Yo también ecribo cuentos*" ("I Also Write Tales"), and in "*Otras escrituras*" ("Other Writings"), "*Sobre la poesía*" ("About Poetry"), "*Literaturas*" ("Literatures"), "*Siempre la poesía*" ("Always Poetry"), and "*La poesía otra vez*" ("Poetry Again")—to cite poems with the most eloquent titles—the countless poets Gelman mentions shape his ideological universe.

Many of them are mentioned in "*Ruiseñores de nuevo*." There is Verlaine and his relationship with music; the youth of Rimbaud; the wisdom of Blake; John Donne's underworld; Martí cultivating a white rose; Walt Whitman with a nightingale on his shoulder; Apollinaire and his calligrams; Baudelaire and his correspondences; Saint John of the Cross and his living flame of love. All these poets name Gelman's preoccupations and longings. All of them construct his poetic image and personality and define his place in the poetic world. All of them form an "I," the "I" of the poetry, the poetic "I" of Gelman cleaved in exile. All these poetic identities contain and define him.

In his acceptance speech of the Miguel de Cervantes Prize on November 28, 2007, Gelman discloses more clues about his ethical-genealogical tree of poetry:

> Sappho spoke of the beautiful orchard . . . Mallarmé met
> the nudity of scattered dreams, Saint Teresa picked the

> images and phantoms of the objects that shake the appetite, Saint John drank the wine of love that only a glass serves, Cavalcanti envisioned a woman who made the air tremble with her clarity, Hidegarda de Bingen cried the soft tears of compunction, and such beauty charged with life causes tremors of the whole being. Wouldn't it be the dream of another dream the poetic word?

The poets elected here have revolutionized poetry, becoming paradigms from their interventions: Saint John of the Cross with his mystical and at the same time amatory poetry, Baudelaire as the father of modern poetry, Tzara the main mentor of the Dadaist movement and questioner of meaning, and Sappho as the first poetess who focuses her love on the female body.

These poets define an inner circle that shapes Gelman's poetic identity. This is a circle where admiration coexists with the convocation of dialogue. But also, the fight or dispute for a place in history is present as well as the attempt to surpass what has come down as a poetic inheritance. Gelman admires his poets, but he also challenges them, correcting them and inviting new appraisals of their old preoccupations and obsessions.

Politically Committed Poetry

The tango's lyrical philosophy exercised on the young locals of the 1950s, a sort of hypnotism that would later transmute later into committed political poetry. In this period of time, Juan Gelman is a restless middle-class young man who incorporates popular art like the tango into his aesthetic experiences:

> I was a fifteen-year-old boy of common origin who went to the *milonga* with the boys of the neighborhood. I critically incorporated the tango in a natural way, not intellectually preconceived.[257]

The tango developed a system of values and aptitudes that constituted a formal scheme of organization for the *porteños*. The tango established a strong paradigm that many young people followed as if it were a religion.

It was an aesthetic revolution, but it was also like a profession of faith, a priesthood, a school, and a form of life. With its own codes, it defined the limits and terms of coexistence, romance, family, injustice, and defense of honor before an affront.

The tango requested an active attitude at that time, like a sort of position in front of life itself. In many cases, it had to be defended to the opposing parties that wielded a strong rivalry. These were the years of the dialectic confrontations between those who adored Osvaldo Pugliese's orchestra and the followers of Juan D'Arienzo:

> I was a *milonga* man since I was fifteen. In that world, then, I was very interested in dance. Borges says that the tango is a way of walking. I'm not going to correct him, but it seems to me like a way of conversing. It is the best way to initiate a good conversation with a woman you don't know. Later the conversation will move to different distinct regions, the dance, and the inevitable questions about each other. Therefore, I believe that the *milonga* is a form of conversation, a danceable dialogue.[258]

That early contact with the existential and loving lyrical poetry of the tango also brought with it a decisive enthusiasm for Colloquialism, a literary movement that became a trend in the progressive circles of the 1960s and was very much adopted by the *tangueros*. Colloquialism arose because of the strong changes the region experienced in the cultural, political and social order. The Cuban Revolution and the nine years of Peronism in Argentina were two of the period's stunning cultural changes. The new literary aesthetic—driven by the most important referents of the Communist Party—proposed a new poetic style based on a colloquial approach. It was a writing style situated far from metaphor and digression. In contrast, it was writing that preferred and promoted a seemingly lineal narrative syntax that opened a path which until then was unexplored in local poetry. It was also politically committed, with a fresh bold tone and strokes of humor and sarcasm.

With that new strategy, the language's rigidity was gradually eliminated, and colloquial forms were incorporated into written poetry. The ideas of purity and aestheticism, developed by the vanguard poetry at the end of the 1940s until the middle of the 1950s, changed to develop new upcoming elements of the local language. Little by little, the expressive search of sublime art faded away, influenced by more ideological content and a less hermetic voice. Poet and critic Daniel García Helder explained this process:

> The social-historical context is reflected in a fashion more and more clear in the poems. . . . The poets of the 1950s observed the emergence of young poets who not only rejected any priest-like role, but who also claimed themselves as militants. For them, poetry ceased being considered "a sacred writing."[259]

Therefore, the vanguards represented by inventions and surrealism, by the idealizations of poetic labor and the aesthetic eagerness of the art, were left behind. Critic and professor Noé Jitrik expressed it in this way:

> . . . poetry, being expression, must confront, must include and still declare what it alludes to, to whom it is directed, what role you believe you play in the lives of others.[260]

The task of redefining this new poetic development was analyzed and projected in their critical works by Urondo and other theoreticians such as César Fernández Moreno. If Latin American poetry was achieved with the emergence of César Vallejo's personal voice, in Argentina the advent of other political discourses (the Peronist's) gave birth to "social colloquialism."

Gelman expressed the demystification of the lyricism that characterized poetic vanguards of the twentieth century through brevity and realistic elements. He defined his existence as a concrete phenomenon and situated himself in a determined, contemporary, temporal-spatial plane. That definition was unlike his previous creations, in which time and place fluctuated between the idyllic past, the instability of the present, and the uncertain future.

The strategy included not only the link between the poet and his environment; it included the connection that he intended to establish with the commonplace Argentinian language. This approach bursts with poetry linked to surrounding reality, to the point that it was considered and denominated in some circles as a "hypersocial" or "neopopular" poetry because of its constant compromise with common urban linguistic reality.

This new approach recovered some of the brilliant rhetorical methods utilized by movements of the beginning of the nineteenth and twentieth centuries in the River Plate region. I refer to the vanguard of gaucho literature and of Sencillism, respectively. Gelman's work was inspired by a variety of schools and literary traditions; it took as much from Sencillism by Baldomero Fernández Moreno (1886–1950) as from the Boedo School (Escuela de Boedo), where Raúl González Tuñón (1905–1974) excelled. It is also important to highlight the work of other great writers cited by Gelman like Oliverio Girondo (1891–1967) and, of course, Juan L. Ortiz (1896–1978).

These discursive strategies, rhetorical methods, and influences formed part of the intent of a movement that represented the values of a new moral conscience. Conversational poetry, combined with all the rich imagery provided by colloquial realism, shaped the two great pillars of his poetry, situating Gelman in a privileged place within the history of Argentinian poetry.

This "new realism," as some have called it, incorporated the least of the rhetoric of the Antipoetic movement and rejected all forms of previous realism. Because neither naturalism, as it emerged from bourgeois realism, nor the Socialist realism promoted particularly by the governments of the Union of Soviet Socialist Republics would form the preferential part of Gelman's poetic framework.

Gelman's major contribution to the later vanguard movement can be seen in what later became known as Latin American politically committed literature. Among the writers associated with this type of poetry, Gelman especially prefers those Latin Americans who, like Nicanor Parra (Chile 1914), Ernesto Cardenal (Nicaragua 1925), Javier Heraud (Peru 1942–1963), Enrique Lihn (Chile 1929–1988), Antonio Cisneros (Peru 1942–2012), Roberto Fernández Retamar (Cuba 1930), Jorge Enrique Adoum (Ecuador 1926–2009), and Roque Dalton (El Salvador 1935–1975), continue the tradition of exposure and social commitment.

Gelman's Six Pseudonyms

Gelman used pseudonyms to diversify his poetic voice, thereby allowing himself to approach his literature in diverse ways, looking for new expressive landscapes. The first to make use of the heteronyms' strategy was the Portuguese Fernando Pessoa, who wrote numerous books that he signed with different names.

Throughout his literary career, Gelman used six different fictitious names to sign his writings. John Wendell, Dom Pero Gonçalvez, Yamanokuchi Ando, Sidney West, José Galván, and finally, Julio Grecco were all masculine pseudonyms used by Gelman as a hallmark.

His first use of fictitious names appeared in 1965, with the second edition of *Cólera buey*. In this book, which includes more than two thousand poems, Gelman introduces three pseudonyms.

In the ninth section of this book, titled "Traducciones I. Los poemas de John Wendell" (Translations I. Poems by John Wendell), there are twenty-nine poems with diverse themes, that, according to Gelman, he translated from a British poet named John Wendell. Gelman created this fictional author whom he makes appear to be real to create distance from what he wrote. The pseudonym offered the independence and ease that the author needed to display contemporary characteristics of his expressiveness. In an interview for *Brecha*, Gelman explained some of the reasons that led him to design this strategy:

> I had locked myself into an intimacy from which I could not

> escape, but then one day I told myself: "Intimacy is fine, it is important, it is part of the subjectivity, but not all subjectivity. I'm going to create a poet to see what comes out of it." It was years from working around the same issue, the same topic, so I ended up inventing these gentlemen. The first one to appear was the British, who wrote five hundred poems which, thanks to God, the police took away in a search; then came the Japanese and the last was Sidney West, the Yankee, which was published first.

The strategy would become more complicated with the inclusion of a second pseudonym. The second part of the ninth section of *Cólera buey*, presented under the name "Los poemas de Dom Pero" ("Poems by Dom Pero"), consisted of three poems that John Wendell attributed to a Portuguese poet named Dom Pero Gonçalvez. In this part, the complexity of the mirrors game increases. Here is John Wendell who, as an intermediary, transmits and transcribes the verses of Dom Pero. Thus, Dom Pero, it might be assumed, was the pseudonym of Wendell, who in turn was the pseudonym of Gelman.

This degree of delegation and exchange in this astonishing game of mirrors provides the best scenario for Gelman to test the use of a particular Spanish, a *sui generis* Spanish. In a rather nondescript Spanish, "in a Spanish that will be seen," as Gelman suggests enigmatically, this pseudonym—Dom Pero, presumably from Lusitanian origin—shaped this dialectal variety of Spanish as if it were part of a staging of an old-time period.

In the poem titled "CDLVI," what appears to be a chronicle of the European conquests and settlements in the north of Argentina, are mentioned customs of the inhabitants of this region, including nakedness of the man ("mansos avestruces que criamos en casa/ donde ya no tapamos nuestras vergüenzas") (meek ostriches that we raise at home/ where we do not cover our shame), women's garments ("las mujeres se cubren todavía con manta pequeña") (the women still cover themselves with small blankets), and their languages ("gritan/ en toncoté indama zanavirona y lule grita") (they shout/ in toncoté indama sanavirona and lule shout). Dom Pero's text closely follows some descriptions that appear in the book written by the historian Vicente Fidel López entitled *Historia de la República Argentina* (*History of Argentina's Republic*):

> The general language that the Indians spoke in those provinces was the *diaguita,* although there were others called *tonozote, indama, zanavirona* and *lule.* The men covered their shame with ostriches' feathers; the women with small aprons knitted with wool or hay, *after the Christians entered that territory,* all were generally dressed in wool and cotton, as influenced by Indians from Peru.[261]

The poem, which opens with innocent images, ends up becoming a testimony against subjugation in the final verses: "idólatras . . . una quedará/ para encander el rencor y las brasas" (somebody will remain/ to ignite the grudge and the grills).

Dom Pero becomes a perfectly designed tool created by Gelman to speak of a distant era where the chronicles of the conquest and Iberian expansion in South America were the preferred texts of the time. As seen at the end of the poem, Gelman does not abandon his ideological and anti-imperial position, expressed on this occasion by the Portuguese poet.

Cólera buey will also be the selected book for the third pseudonym. In the section entitled "Traducciones II. Los poemas de Yamanokuchi Ando" (Translations II. Poems by Yamanokuchi Ando), Gelman gives life to a nonexistent Japanese poet for the reasons he explains in the following interview:

> He emerged from a surrealist Japanese poet who existed: Yaminokuchi Baku, whom I read in French, from the school of Okinawa. His poems have nothing to do with the ones I wrote. Yaminokuchi Ando was a deviation, and with ironies and passion I wrote my book. In a decade birthday shift, something grabbed me really bad with the feeling of death.[262]

The idea of engaging in this personification of supposed foreign poets seemed to suggest, as critiques have indicated, that Gelman was attempting to distance the reader from his previous work. He forces readers to ask themselves about the origins of these poets. This strategy also allows other points of view, an opening to other perceptions without the weight of a household name (Gelman) attached and without expecting a stylistic and thematic continuity or sequels.

This emotional distance is what produced Brechtian estrangement or *verfremdungseffekt*, and finally the desired self-referential questions. Gelman was convinced that his production could qualify as intimate until the seventies and that such intimate condition would end by "drowning his poetry," as he pointed out to Mario Benedetti in an interview. The poet opened himself to new and foreign verbal territories, such as the ones that the British John Wendell or the Portuguese Dom Pero opened for him. This intellectual and emotional distance, says María Ángeles Pérez López in the anthology *Oficio ardiente* (*Ardent Career*), aims to "avoid the emotional empathy with his own speech and enable new forms of relationship with poetic matters."

The fourth instance in which Gelman employed this technique was in his sixth book, *Traducciones III: Los poemas de Sidney West* (*Translations III: Poems by Sidney West*). The title reveals a deliberate continuity with the poetry of *Cólera buey*. Within days of publication, Gelman had an immediate corroboration that his stratagem worked perfectly.

> In the weekly magazine where I worked by the end of the seventies, there was one who acted as if he were very literate. One day he told me: "I bought the book *Los poemas de Sidney West* and I read it. We already know what kind of poet Sidney West is, but I just wanted to tell you that I was delighted by your translations." My trick worked.[263]

Traducciones III: Los poemas de Sidney West is composed of a group of twenty "biographic lamentations," or sorrows, that take place in an American geographic context, with an additional poem that closes the series, entitled "Fe de erratas" ("Errata Sheet"). Throughout the sequence, anguish for a big loss and death are most significant. On a secondary level, other minor losses appear like unrecoverable illusions, good old times, and lost passion. The twenty poetic minibiographies included by Gelman can be considered funeral elegies that give notice to the death of various lyrical voices. Thus, he alludes to death countless times. The following examples mentioned the death of Gallagher Bentham ("cuando gallagher bentham murió") (when gallagher bentham died), Butch Butchanam ("hasta que supo que iba a morir") (until he knew he was going to die), Chester Carmichael ("chester carmichael muerto en el otoño de 1962") (Chester Carmichael who died in the autumn of 1962), Stanley Hook ("esa noche naturalmente stanley hook se murió") (that night stanley hook naturally died), Cab Cunningham ("toda la biografía atada por cab cunningham/ crepitó libre cuando él murió") (the whole biography tied by cab cunningham/ crackled freely when he died), Raf Maloney ("cuando raf maloney murió lo cortaron al pájaro") (when raf maloney died they cut him like a bird), and Mecha Vaugham ("no la dejó vivir y cuando mecha vaugham murió") (didn't let her live and when mecha vaugham died), to cite a few examples.

As shown, the use of lowercase letters for personal names forms part of the poet's decision to set the deprived environment where the lives of these characters elapse. To this is added the selection of the places where the penuries of his characters occur, locations that emphasize the torn atmosphere of the texts: those twenty laments elapse between Chicago, Cincinnati, Spoker Hill, Melody Spring, Ginger Street, Hereby Street, Cochrane Street, Oak, Cerville, Louisiana, Dakota, Toledo, Ohio, Alabama, Santa Monica, and other locations. All these places appear contaminated and gloomy with bleak afternoons, where it is easy to get lost and aimlessly stay, where all hope collapses.

> from bucolic springs and Ginger Street[264]
>
> it rained years and years on the pavement of Hereby
> Street[265]
>
> the neighborhood of Spoker Hill had come to hate it[266]
>
> the surges (snake-like) of the time in Melody Spring
>
> david cassidy will find himself stranded in Cochrane
> Street[267]
>
> in the ferocious afternoons in Ohio[268]
>
> in the dirty morning of Santa Monica
> because of the soot, the exhaust pipe
> the crushed dreams, rotten from last night[269]

Despite the melancholic atmosphere of those poetic moments, there is always room for something to be saved. In Gelman's poetry, there would always be a bird ready to sing the poetry of life, in the form of a lament, a dirge, or an elegy.

> it was learned that the eyes of vernon vries lived like this:
> worshiping birds rivers falls and the vast ocean[270]

The recurring image of the birds is placed on the list of things worshiped by the poet, such as nature and beauty. The bird could well represent the song of the poet, the beautiful expression, i.e., poetry.

But the text does not lessen its complexity in those gloomy scenes. In one of the poems of Sidney West, "Lamento por el uteró de mecha vaugham" ("Lament for the Uterus of Mecha Vaugham"), a feminine voice reads and recites fragments of the poem "Si," included by Gelman in the second section of *Cólera buey*. Thus the sequence develops as follows: Sydney West poetizes aspects of Mecha Vaugham's experience which, as it is read, she identifies with the views of Gelman, the one who gives poetic life to Sidney West. The circularity becomes excessive. The excess overrides the effect, and the veil of the pseudonyms falls. The resource is depleted, and the urgent necessity of exposing oneself emerges. Then, the moment to enunciate what is real and truthful has come.

If there were any doubt, in "Fe de erratas," Sidney West writes that he was eaten by all the birds that he invented ("sidney west se lo comieron todos los pájaros que supo inventar"), as if he were some sort of Don Quixote who is dominated and beaten by his own imagery and inventions. The unveiled poetic voice favors rebirth of the poetry that expands the hopes and continuously restarts. Maybe that is why the series closes with "Fe de erratas," an open invocation for Sidney (the "creator" of this lament) to sleep and abandon the world of the funeral elegies for a while: "que duerma duerma duerma/ que duerma sidney west" (sleep sleep sleep/ sleep sidney west).

The fifth and sixth opportunities where the strategy of the mirror is displayed is in *Hacia el sur*, Gelman's sixteenth book of poems, which consists of four sections. The piece that was written in Rome between 1981 and 1982 works with imagery oriented to a very specific place:

the South. The composition is very concrete, "la pizzería del sur" (the pizza place from the South), but also highly idealized, "te amo/señora/como al Sur" (I love you/lady/like the South). This predisposes the perfect setting, mythological and real, where ghosts born in the exile are exorcised. The idea of South will give logic to the mixture that is the mechanism underlying this book. The combination of materials of different extraction or tradition open in these pages as if it were a tailor's coffin, where Argentinian slang, the tango, and the River Plate region merge with angels, victims, assassins, combs, and the spirit of the poetry itself. From that collage arises a mythical construction of the homeland notion, the homeland of the far South.

The second section that comprises the book, "The Poems of José Galván," is preceded by a clarification signed by Gelman. According to "Noticias" ("News"), the poems in this section were written by a *desaparecido*, a missing person, a victim of state terrorism.

> News
>
> It is my duty to publish these poems that came to me by chance or miracle. Their author disappeared in late 1978 in Argentina, murdered or kidnaped by the military dictatorship. His imprisonments and exiles under other dictatorships were known, as well as a handful of poems that he published in discontinued old literary magazines from the city of Buenos Aires.[271]

It seems disturbing that what at first seems to be a truthful circumstance in Argentina at the time, the kidnapping and disappearance of the poet José Galván, becomes during the reading another literary device Gelman uses to display his new concerns. In this case, Gelman's poetic reality is formed by a duet of voices.

The same happens in the last section, "Los poemas de Julio Grecco" ("The Poems of Julio Grecco"), that is preceded by a "Report" signed by José Galván.

> Julio Greco fell fighting against the military dictatorship on October 24, 1976. I kept these poems for him. José Galván. Buenos Aires/1978.[272]

Again, the complexity increases: Gelman gathers verses of a certain José Galván who at the same time retrieves some poems from the anonymity of Julio Grecco, a hypothetical Argentinian zealot. The double mirror that finally emerges when one understands the enormous similarities between the poems and biographies of these three "poets" corresponds to the game of pseudonyms also used by Gelman in "Translations I," "Translations II," and the book *Translations III.* The poetic similarity between the three opens the door to a critical remark that we consider opportune to reveal.

Pseudonyms or Heteronyms?

As much as in the poems attributed to John Wendell as in the ones attributed to Dom Pero Gonçalvez, Yamanokuchi Ando, Sidney West, José Galván, and Julio Grecco, there is a common element: they all serve as pseudonyms of Gelman, not as heteronyms.

Specialized critique has understood for years that Gelman, like Pessoa, used the resource of heteronyms. However, the strategies are subtly different. The fundamental difference prevails in the autonomy and independence of the created poet.

It is known that Fernando Pessoa is the great poet of multiple heteronyms; his attempt was to conceal or depersonalize himself in the figures of personalities or alter egos, shaping by this route the breath and complexity of his thoughts, knowledge, and perceptions of life and world. Pessoa's heteronyms have been seen as the expression of different facets of Fernando Pessoa's personality and the manifestation of a profound imagination.

Pessoa always manifested that his heteronyms were to be read as independent poets of himself. To Pessoa, heteronyms are demarcated by his spiritual integrity; they are "beings" living inside him, although he consciously participates in the elaboration of his most peculiar characteristics; each one has a literal life and destiny independent of its author.

The biographies of Pessoa's heteronyms are armed with vast amounts of detail. Three are the fundamental heteronyms with which Pessoa signed the work that he didn't publish under his own name: Alberto Caeiro, Ricardo Reis, and Álvaro de Campos. The three of them were endowed by their creator not only a date of birth and biography, but also diverse personal characteristics that made them recognizable. Caeiro, the master of the other two, was a self-thought sensualist and agnostic sage who lived in close contact with nature. Reis, to whom Saramago dedicated one of his novels, was a humanist and pagan poet, disciple of Horacio and Anacreonte, archaic in his poetry, with a marked monarchic ideology. Álvaro de Campos, perhaps the most artistically valuable of all of them, was a British naval engineer, fascinated by the same things as the futurists—speed, engines, the ever-changing world—and strongly influenced by the poetry of Walt Whitman. For each of these men, Fernando Pessoa designed a careful biography, horoscope, complete physical picture; he traced their moral, intellectual, and ideological characteristics: three different characters, each with a distinct literary activity.

The strategy of Gelman is different. As much in the case of José Galván as in the case of Julio Grecco, Wendell, West, Pero Gonçalvez, and Ando, that degree of biographical independence does not exist.

Both Galván and Grecco, to name two of the last pseudonyms created by Gelman, have many things in common with Gelman: the three of them are Argentinian, political activists, and poets. They share initials (J. G.) and fathers. In "Verdades" ("Truths"), one of Gelman's pseudonyms writes about his father, a Ukrainian who takes refuge in a wooden house in Moscow while escaping from the Tsarist forces.

> I don't know what my Ukrainian father in England
> would do/. . .
> he is at the wooden house in Moscow from which he
> will escape/ because it is the year 1905/
> and that revolution failed/ and dad's skin failed/[273]

As seen, Gelman and these two pseudonyms share a paternal biography. As remembered, profuse allusions appear to the biography of Gelman's father in *Bajo la lluvia ajena (notas al pie de una derrota).*

XII[274]

> My father came to South America with a hand behind his back and another one in front, to have his pants high up in his waist. I came to Europe with a soul in my back and another in front, to have my pants high up in my waist. There are differences, however: he went there to stay, I came here to go back.

They also share similar poetic styles. In the thematic order, there are recurrences that clearly refer to Gelman's imagery. In both Galvan's and Grecco's work, the remembrance of the fallen *compañeros* is still present:

> . . . like the *compañeros*
> who fought calmly and with disdain/
> they sought many victories/
> moons to live once and for all[275]

In these compositions, one can observe the same need to remember the names of reporters and Gelman's poet colleagues like Rodolfo Walsh and Paco Urondo; one curiously disappeared like Galván, and the other died in combat like Grecco.

> also, this hand that flows over there
> has the warmth of Paco/ of his cheek that this hand
> once dried
> when treason filled it with tears
> of magdalene for christ/[276]

The new semantic of the word *South* that acquires the sense of homeland and belonging is constant in both series.

> with branches open to the South/
> bound with herbs of the universe/
> but always in the South/ South of the South/ where
> the cordillera harbors/ the pampas sing like the sea[277]

Neither the topics nor the procedures used by these poets differ. Both Galván and Grecco appeal to the same formal and stylistic devices that Gelman used in his previous books: interversal pause ("entre las 5 y las 7/ cada día"*)* (between 5 and 7/ each day); enjambments ("cuando te conocí/ mi corazón tenía más hambre que piojo de peluca") (when I knew you/ my heart was hungrier than lice on a wig); conversion of a noun to a verb (*amañanarte*) (to fix you); presence of diminutives (*fueguitos, hojita, almita, telitas)* (little fires, little leaf, little soul, little fabrics); use of poliptoton, the repetition of a word with different meanings, ("mano que mana") (the hand that flows); rhetorical questions ("¿qué estás haciendo con tu cuerpo?/¿separándolo/ de la muerte?/¿juntándolo con ella/la graciosa/ llena de noches que miraron su cuello y se quedaron ahí?/ ¿qué pasa con sus almas?/¿la almita de tu alma?") (what are you doing with your body?/separating it/from death?/joining it with her/ the graceful/ full of nights of looking at her neck and staying there?/what happens with their souls?/the little soul of your soul?), among other devices.

For all these reasons, it is more accurate to speak of semiheteronyms or simply pseudonyms, but not of heteronyms. This position is confirmed by Gelman in an interview in the newspaper, *Clarín,* in 2000.

> . . . I use two types of pseudonyms that never were heteronyms like Pessoa. I needed the firsts—John Wendell, Yamanokuchi Ando, Sidney West—to move away from myself. The seconds—José Galván, Julio Grecco—to reunite me with my losses.[278]

In conclusion, these pseudonyms signify to Gelman a necessary path, not a mere literary resort. Through these, Gelman reveals his usual old concerns, but from an unfamiliar perspective and with a new intimacy.

The Last Journey

At the end of his life, the doctors suggested to Gelman that he return to receive chemotherapy treatment. Gelman refused. He wanted to travel to Buenos Aires to present his final book and say goodbye to his country. From the outset, he agreed with his wife that there should be no effort to try to prolong a life that was fading. He rejected drugs, radiation treatments, and surgery. He wanted to die in his house in Mexico with his loved ones, away from hospitals and the medical bureaucracy. He wrote until his last moment. He still had things that he needed to say.

The dawn of August 20, 2013, in Buenos Aires, Gelman told his friend, Horacio Verbitsky, that the end was near, that he must say goodbye, and that it was time to thank him before leaving. Verbitsky described the meeting:

> Juan takes me by the shoulder and speaks to me softly. Lucila Pagliai (who participates in ANCLA, Agencia de Noticias Clandestina [Clandestine News Agency], the underground news agency founded by Rodolfo Walsh at the beginning of the dictatorship) sees us but doesn't hear our dialogue . . . It is the last time that we meet. Fifty years have passed since the first time. Death arrives six months from this moment: Mara informed us that Juan had approached the finish line. "It is

> imminent, it can be several days, it can be hours." I asked if he was conscious. "Yes. But he doesn't have a voice and is fading away." And finally: "Perro, Juan died an hour and a quarter ago."[279]

Days before dying, he wrote one of his more explicit and poignant poems, "Verdad es" ("Truth is"), written on October 28 and finished this way:

> Looted skeleton, soon nothing will clutter your view/
> fickleness. You will bear/ the naked universe.[280]

Goodbye and Farewell

It is the time of day in which one turns off the light and silence empowers the scene. There aren't extensions, nor deferments. The nonsense takes over the event which goes around the world. There is no necessity for explanations. "Let it go, Juan"—Walt Whitman would have said—and Juan let it go. His life is gone. He surrenders to the mystery of death, searching other universes, the depths of souls. He no longer wanted any more. . . . Finally, he said what no one thought he would say . . . He said the end.

CXCIV

> The lark did not want to get dirty/ it said enough/ it said
> end. It said enough/ it did not want to get dirty/ it said
> end. Raised to write its gift of flight / it said enough. It
> leaked when said enough in alleys of known darkness/
> strokes of madness. It was surprised and said end/ they
> killed everything around / it said enough. It opened
> bolts of evil / flashes of the angry heart / it said end.
> The lark said end.[281]

On Tuesday, January 14, 2014, at 4:30 p.m., Juan Gelman died of a sickness called myelodysplasia syndrome in his house in the Condesa colony in Mexico City. He was eighty-three years old. His life and his work leave testimony of his struggle.

CXLIII

> In the fear of death, death is not worth it. The afflicted are not interesting, nor those crippled by love, nor the portentous wit of a summer. What is important is the light received in the form of entrails to see oneself. The sensation of the body that ends does not live in a closed corner, it creates its double in impalpable seasons and aliquots of sorrow without notary. A calandra lark organizes the failure of a spent match.[282]

The spent match, this time, couldn't be ignited. The international press echoed the news. Death interests, just as the aliquots of pain and earned awards, intrigues and attracts.

The news traveled fast in the capital of Mexico, one of his adopted cities. The newspaper *Milenio*, in which Gelman wrote a weekly column, reported that the poet died in his home: "He died peacefully, in his home, surrounded by his family." Organizations and literary institutions of Mexico felt the impact of the news of his death and said goodbye to the poet. Gelman had collaborated regularly with the directors and executives of these groups: Rafael Tovar y de Teresa, president of the National Council for Culture and the Arts; María Cristina García Cepeda, director of the Institute of Fine Arts; Marisol Schultz, director of the International Book Fair of Guadalajara; writer Benito Taibo II; journalist Jenaro Villamil; the director of the Library of Mexico, and the publishing company, El Naranjo; all showed their regret for the loss.

The Argentinian government decreed three days of national mourning and ordered that the flag remain at half-mast on all public buildings in memory of the poet.

Also, the Uruguayan government, through its Ministry of Foreign Affairs, expressed sorrow and stated that "Gelman has been a sensitive and committed individual his entire life."

The Spanish newspaper *El País* confirmed Gelman's will to cling to a life that he felt no longer belonged to him. The Spanish government, through its president, also regretted the death of Gelman, an "irreplaceable" voice of the "turbulent twentieth century."

Ashes of Nepantla

On January 18, 2014, the remains of the poet were scattered from a bridge that crosses the Mexican town of San Miguel Nepantla, the same location from which Sor Juana Inés de la Cruz, so admired by Gelman, originated. The secretary of Culture of the City of Mexico, Eduardo Vázquez Martín, recalled the emotional ceremony: "It was a celebration of Juan's life; we read some of his poems, we drank wine, and we ate roasted chicken, avocados, tomatoes and oil, always accompanied by the song of the Mexican *jaranas* and the Buenos Aires accent of our expatriates of the South. . . . The sun warmed the border between the cold forests of the Mexican state and the cane fields of Morelos."[283]

Death as a Theme

In the year 2007, at seventy-seven years of age, Gelman began to give more space in his poetry to the theme of death. What had initially appeared to be an emerging concern in *Mundar* would become more present, urgent, and insistent as his disease progressed. This was especially obvious in *De atrásalante en su porfía.* At the end of the trail, in his last book *Hoy* (*Today*), the theme of mourning was manifested in a more natural way. Gelman seemed to accept and understand most of the condition of mortality.

In *Mundar*, his twenty-seventh book, published in 2007, the theme of death constantly appears. The first textual encounter with mourning is the first manifestation of the question of one's own death in "Paco," a poem dedicated to Francisco "Paco" Urondo. As is imaginable, the issue of death brings an inevitable and solemn disturbance. "Nos veremos"[284] (We will meet again), Gelman says to an already dead Paco Urondo. Death occurs daily "Habrás/ hablado mucho con tu muerte"[285] (You would have/ talked so much with your death) and at the same time, is an unfathomable mystery, "Qué hay por allí"[286] (What is out there?).

Death as a substantial issue is closely linked to the theme of time. The past of the poet emerges, as expected, surrounding the question of time. Therefore, he frequently mentioned the past ("El pasado vuelve")[287] (The past returns); a future that already happened (". . . obligaremos al futuro a volver otra vez")[288] (. . .we will force the future to return again), which evidently entails a vision of pessimism, in addition to allusions of the simultaneity of time ("Hoy viene mañana como ayer")[289] (Today comes tomorrow like yesterday).

With the perspective acquired through the years, the past appears like an arid, remote, vast, and painful territory.

> Defeat/ I read your book
> close teacher/ already free[290]

If the question of time is derived from the theme of death, the attention ends by focusing on the very same nothingness. Nothingness, named in numerous opportunities, would seem to approach an existential and unexplored abyss.

> where? / went the ombú tree that on you grew/…
> where will the words that could not be born go? /…
> in which void did they enter?[291]

Death, named in a direct or veiled form, like when the poet uses the existential theme, mentioning nothingness and emptiness, will have a notable presence in the poems.

In his following two books of poems, this emerging concern "tomo ocho medicamentos por día para que la muerte me espere más tarde"[292] (I took eight medications a day for death to wait for me a little longer), will be carefully reworked until his last days.

Gelman's twenty-eighth book of poetry, *De atrásalante en su profía*, published in 2011, is composed of 155 poems where death forms one of the central thematic categories. We find there a vast diversity of issues and concerns; but death is the one that appears most strongly, especially in the final part. Nothingness, a theme that continues from the disquisitions of his previous book, and the issue of past time appear as variants of the tragic theme.

Death is a realistic possibility for a man of eighty. In "La huella" ("Sleuth"), the poetic subject says that there are "cuerpos que temen a la muerte/ y desean morir" (bodies that fear death/ and wish to die). In "Baile" ("Dance"), he goes even further, understanding that life is a dispensable item: "Amarte es preciso, vivir no" (To love you is necessary, to live is not). In this way, a new perspective of the tragic theme will be inaugurated.

What at first seemed worrisome in *Mundar* now results in a greater urgency. It is as if Gelman wanted to talk about his death from a place of absolute intellectual honesty. He is not denied by the evident, the real possibility of death; he does not fall into the taboo of avoiding talking about the issue nor does he address it through subterfuge or euphemisms. Death can also be a choice, the desire to crown the best means possible at the end of a tour.

Gelman names the unnamable, conjures the ghosts and the naked will of the poet. In the words of Horacio Verbitsky, Gelman "Jamás se permitió un engaño, ni siquiera una verdad a medias"[293] (never allowed a hoax, not even a half-truth).

Who

Who encloses the twilight in his fear
looks for animals that
will eat him, bon appetit.
To paint one's soul is an
anatomical situation that moves away
the self from truth, the life from
its storms and new sorrows born, circles
synthesis of emptiness, courts[294]

Concealed carnivorous animals—suggests the poet—awake when "being away from the truth." Neither taboos, nor costumes, nor paintings will unmask the truth. The goal of his poetry is naming what is necessary, in the most direct possible way.

On the other hand, the subject of death recalls other issues such as reflection on the past. From his perspective, the future is a brief and unpredictable instance, now more than ever. The past, meanwhile, is shown as a vast territory populated by hundreds of characters and voices. The shelter provided by the return to the past can be a comfort. It can be a way to enable a new vision of the future, a way of looking back in order to follow the path ahead. In Gelman's terms, it represents "el salto para atrásalante" (the back-and-forth jump) that is mentioned in the poem "Des."[295]

However, this look back, this retrospective jump can also be painful, especially when the presence of the past was not as he had dreamed: "cicatrices/ de lo que nunca fue" (scars/ of what never happened) he says in "Animales" ("Animals"). The revelation brings with it a sense of frustration and despair. The balance is impossible, or in the best case, highly unfavorable. This becomes true especially when one believes that the path taken in the past is inhabited by the ghosts of nonexistence, as he implies in "Lluvia" ("Rain"): "Campos/ de lo que no hubo no habido" (Fields/ of what there wasn't not been).

The return to the past brings the most enormous revelation: an imperfect past, a past different from the dream. "La mano que golpea la puerta de lo que no pasó"[296] (The hand that strikes the door of what did not happen) is the same hand that draws the veil of death, hitherto hidden. The past is no longer a retreat. Revelation is hopeless. The passage of time is a "slope," each time growing steeper. In "Fuga" ("Escape"), the past appears elusive, slippery, hard to remember: "le huye al papel" (it runs away from the paper). Voices lose color; they will "fade" and the past that emerges grows faint quickly, becoming nothing more than a disheartening hallucination: "tu sangre abierta en mí"[297] (your blood opens in me). Therefore, no escape was reached, only pain and truth—as it reads in "Teoría" ("Theory").

In the
waiting room of his train
the old dreams pass

every day they open
with a currency that does not exist.[298]

The past times and the "old dreams" unveil a nonexistent reality, "una moneda que no existe" (a currency that does not exist) that paradoxically is evoked "every day."

Hoy, the thirtieth and last book published while Gelman was still alive, is composed of a selection of poems written during 2011 and 2012. It includes almost three hundred poems that roam various topics, sorted and ordered by roman numerals, with the exception of the last poem, which takes a nonnumeric and enigmatic title that we will discuss later in greater detail.

From the title of the new book, one of the central themes of the work becomes clear: time. The subject of time, a scarce resource, concentrated on various concerns. First, the concept "today" has a double face. On one hand, it can be understood as a circumscribed period of twenty-four hours. Nevertheless, what we now call "today," tomorrow will be "yesterday," and what we now call "tomorrow" becomes "today." In other words, the word refers to something that constantly evolves. "Today" is now, no doubt about it, but tomorrow will also be "today," and the day after will become "today." The progression of time does not mean having to invoke a new word. Therefore, the choice of "today" speaks of an immediate and urgent time (clock), but also an eternal time, suspended in an endless season. "Today" is haste, but is also constancy and permanence, a permanence that one day ceases to be, exactly the day of his death: "el día que no vino más" (the day that no longer came), says Gelman in "XCIII."

Time, on the other hand, has specific derivations: These include nostalgia about the past which once was lived as "today," and the uncertain future that future generations will live as a successive crowd of many "todays."

In *De atrásalante en su profía,* we indicated the strong presence of the theme of death in Gelman's work. The "To love you is necessary, to live is not" from "Baile," which we mentioned, is a good example. The period of time when Gelman wrote his book appears to coincide with the acknowledgement of his disease. From then until the end of his life, with an increasingly acute health picture, Gelman seems to understand more precisely the issue of death, perhaps because, as he says in "VII," "Pensar la muerte cambia a la muerte" (Thinking about death changes the death).

Therefore, for this specific issue, *De atrásalante en su profía* and his latest collection of poems, *Hoy,* establish a permanent dialogue. The issue that arises as an unstoppable force in the 2009 book seems appeased, finding peace and acceptance in the proposal of *Hoy*: "En el miedo a la muerte la muerte no vale la pena" (In the fear of death, death is not worth it). What once concerned and was not rationally understood then appears more clearly today, as natural and accepted: "La muerte vino a darles la razón"[299] (Death came to prove them right). The ignorance about postmortem fate is no longer a concern. It is now about how to leave this world in the best possible way: "canta cómo irse mejor." There are no more questions, but acceptance and peace: "El pensamiento hace una flor que entretiene a la muerte"[300] (Thought makes a flower that entertains death).

There is a manifest trust in the mystery of life and death: "Prometeo nunca dijo cómo se roba… la muerte al muerto"[301] (Prometheus never says how to steal . . . death from the dead). One's own life is finally offered to the act of singing and to the ritual of farewell: "La tarea de matar a la muerte cabe en una caja chica."[302] (The task of killing death fits into a small box.)

Death is finally accepted without triggering drama: "Llegan los ruidos de la muerte cotidiana"[303] (The everyday noises of death come). Gelman understands death is natural and even necessary: "La vida que se va deja un soplo en medio de la mano que es inútil besar"[304] (The life that goes away leaves a breath in the middle of the hand that is useless to kiss).

His poetry once again closely follows his biography. Gelman expressly established before a notary public that he did not want to prolong his life, if it could only be continued with the help of hospital technology.

For all this, *Hoy* is the beginning and end of a path: "Apagar, apagar, apagar, tómbolas de la muerte/ vine y me voy"[305] (Off, off, off, raffles death / I come and go). *Hoy* is the Gordian knot of Gelmanic poetry. It puts an end to a path of questions and concerns. But it is also the Borgesian Aleph, where all points raised in the earlier poems are concentrated. It is the synthesis of a life and the end of a journey. It is farewell but also the final answer, which is not surprising; there are no answers. Because at the end "hay preguntas muy muertas"[306] (there are very dead questions) and finally, "el vacío abandona todas las conjeturas"[307] (emptiness abandons all conjecture). Nothingness—that is, the absolute absence of everything—is all that's left.

CXXXIII

> Resting on a chair let me see better the destruction
> of a hummingbird. Lying on its death, the color still
> sings, remembers the oblique line of the pass. Now
> still in its beauty that will not last long / enters in
> depths consummated by the desire to embrace the
> entire humanity, stepped into the neck of pain to get
> information about bliss. Hummingbird that leaves in
> dry leaves and a dark ego.[308]

The agony of the hummingbird becomes real in final darkness. Death is the color that leaves, the beauty that does not last and stillness that descends to the depth of sterile desire and dark ego: "El deseo no se quiere morir ante el cadáver del deseo"[309] (The desire doesn't want to die in front of the dead body of desire).

Hoy represents a path to where death, exile, the inflexibility of the words, and his past life are mixed. It is not surprising, therefore, that the thematic quintet (death, son, exile, words, and nothingness) appears so clearly interrelated. All issues continue into each other. Thus, the question of poetry involves nonliterary topics. The dead child is the love that cannot be explained, the fear that is not understood, the past time that did not happen because "La muerte no interpreta sus textos"[310] (Death does not interpret its texts). Nothingness is emptiness. There is nothing to understand: "Vida y muerte se abrazan sin pagar"[311] (Life and death embrace without pay).

But all at once, everything is explained by the absence of an explanation. It is understood that the answer is acceptance and love. It is like the fish that eats its tail but does not fatten with its own meat that is rich and flavorful, because the progression leads to the disappearance, to the same nothingness: teeth eating themselves, stomach that does not digest because it was already devoured. The image implies confusion and a paradox. Perhaps because of this, Gelman closes his last book with the poem titled "Y?" ("And?"), a question that does not close and that appears interrupted. He understands that there is no valid question. Questions appear incomplete because they are incapable of generating the right query that encompasses the complexity of the dynamic of life.

The literary legacy, then, becomes eternal acceptance and peace, the peace of a lifetime that will endure even in death: "La eternidad ha muerto y todo es diferente y se busca en el uno imposible"[312] (Eternity has died and everything is different and it searches itself in the impossible one).

Appendices

I. Testimonies about Juan Gelman

Gelman's work has been appreciated and criticized by hundreds of writers and critics from around the world. The testimonies quoted below highlight fundamental aspects of his personality and work.

"Death lies when it says Juan Gelman is no longer around. . . . He is still alive in all who loved him, in all who read him, in all who have listened to our deepest inside in his voice. . . ." *(Eduardo Galeano)*

"He was a great poet. It is the loss of a poet from all Latin America who also honored us by choosing to live in Mexico. In addition to a great poet, he was a social activist. He was this during his entire life. . . ." *(Elena Poniatowska)*

"Talking about Gelman's work is talking about an internal movement of great commotion in the Spanish poetic language, because it spans a wide register that goes from a wounded emotional world to a historic world seeking an impossible sweetness. In that sense, all Gelman's findings stand out concerning the renewal of the Argentinian poetic diction from the sixties onwards." *(Horacio González)*

“The interest of poetry, its power of revelation, is usually directly proportional to the risks assumed by the poet. In this sense, Juan Gelman has never let us down. . . . Juan knows that Federico García Lorca was killed in Tucumán, in Azul, in Santa Fe, in Salta. We know that Haroldo Conti was killed in Badajoz, that Rodolfo Walsh fell in Teruel, that Francisco Urondo was murdered in Madrid. . . .” *(Jorge Riechmann)*

“I have a hard ear for poetry, but that does not prevent me from identifying it beyond the confines of the verse and the book. That is why, although I recognize the talent of lyrical Gelman, I prefer to call attention to his other poetry: the one he wrote with his life, through his actions and even his silences. Literary works abound in this country. What are not many are incorruptible artists who are or have been examples in life, people who have not bitten the dust when they have been victims of one of the moral trippings that our country practices daily.” *(Marcelo Figueras)*

“The life of Juan Gelman was a ceaseless struggle against State crimes, violence, and injustices. It also turned into a language struggle; a battle that allowed him to write what had never been written nor will be written again.” *(José Emilio Pacheco)*

“My friendship with Gelman was a very bright stage of my youth. . . . Juan ended forever that division between spoken and written language, that thought that certain words could not be used in poetry. . . . I would say that with his decease, the 1960 decade goes away.” *(Juana Bignozzi)*

“As I always say, the spacebar that characterizes his poems is a sutured cut in the verse. It is perhaps a graphic mark, which cannot be vocalized or put into sound; it can only be watched, like a scar. That bar is the signal and the lure of the gap that poetry opens between nature and culture, between pain and ideology, perhaps. But at the same time the bars become his poems, and his entire poetry a wounded and healed body.” *(Arturo Carrera)*

“Gelman comes and goes from the metaphors that he creates and abandons without regrets, from the several versions of the poems in their original tradition, inventing words just to clarify their meanings, from an indirect autobiography and a direct confession, from love and desire and the sense of pure pain, from pure pain . . . " *(Carlos Monsiváis)*

"One time, I formulated the poetic theory from *Luces que a lo lejos*:[313] 'The Argentines are victims of the deception of Gardel. . . . We never go back to the first love. . . . we never ever go back to anything'. . . Juan stayed deep in thought, familiarized with judicial rhetoric for its determined search of their missing, he warned me: 'Such a serious accusation against Gardel needs hard evidence.'" *(Alberto Spunzberg)*

"Writing until the last moment, and dying in your bed, two extraordinary privileges that you well deserved, my friend. I offer you some wild flowers to accompany you, from the people who admired your poems and who loved you personally." *(Diana Bellessi)*

"Gelman made a career in his very original, own language. He has gone through periods of personal suffering, but he has lived them well and has written wonderful poems." *(Noé Jitrik)*

"He's one of the few poets, since César Vallejo, who has been able to join political commitment with linguistic experimentation. . . . What amazes me the most is that Gelman was such a delicately lyrical poet, so radical in his stylistic inquiries. Yet he has always raised very strong ethical concerns in his poems. That is a priceless legacy; I invite everyone to read him." *(Andrés Neuman)*

"He leaves us a legacy of righteous rebellion, and especially the legacy of having a dream of what should be, what could be better and more human. His poetry absolutely corresponds to his dreams and his actions." *(Dolores Castro)*

"We have his powerful, indelible presence in our memory, giving us strength and evidence of what it means to risk life for writing." *(Daniel Freidemberg)*

II. Awards

Gelman's work has been translated into over a dozen languages, among which are English, French, Portuguese, German, Italian, Dutch, Swedish, Hungarian, Czech, Turkish, Chinese, and Japanese. He also received countless awards around the world. Listed below are those of greater public importance.

In 1997, Gelman received the highest distinction reserved for Spanish language poets awarded by the Argentine government, the National Poetry Prize, for his work from 1994 to 1997. The award involves the delivery of $15,000 US and a lifelong pension. At the award ceremony, Gelman denounced the socioeconomic policy of the government of former President Carlos Menem and those "henchmen of the military dictatorship that walk the streets of the country and the public offices with impunity." He dedicated his award to the "living victims" of the dictatorship, "victims who became known as 'missing,' and to those struggling on the Jujuy routes, in the white tents of Buenos Aires," to his son and missing daughter-in-law, and to "the son or daughter of both."

In 2000, he was awarded the Juan Rulfo Literary Prize in Mexico, one of the most prestigious awards in the Spanish language. The award involves the delivery of $100,000 US. The judges meeting in Guadalajara (Jalisco) valued the "admirable fidelity" of the poet with his poetry: "I am encouraged to continue working on the miracle of the creation of the word," said Gelman, upon learning about receiving the award.

The following year, he was honored with the Rodolfo Walsh Prize for his work as a journalist, awarded by the faculty of journalism and communication at the University of La Plata in Argentina.

That year, he also received two awards for his literary career: the Poetry Award di Lerici Pea in Italy, becoming the first Latin American writer to receive this award, and the José Lezama Lima Poetry Prize, issued by Casa de las Américas of Cuba, for his anthology, *Pesar todo.*

In Mexico, where he was admired and respected for imparting new vigor to language, he received the Ramón López Velarde Ibero-American Poetry Prize. He became the first non-Mexican author to gain this award.

In Argentina, he obtained the Buenos Aires Book Fair Award for *País que fue será*, considered the best literary work in 2004. He also gained the Platinum Konex Award for the poetry he produced between 1994 and 1998.

In Chile, he received the Pablo Neruda Ibero-American Poetry Prize that was set the previous year within the frame of the centennial of the National Prize in 2005. This award was established by the Chilean government in 2004 in commemoration of the birthday centennial of the Nobel Prize laureate Pablo Neruda.

In Cuba, Gelman received the Nicolás Guillén Philosophical Literature Prize for his literary work in Italy and Cuba.

In Ávila, Spain, Gelman was awarded *ex aequo*, at the seventieth Teresa de Ávila National Literary Award, receiving €9,016.

On October 28, 2005, he received in Salamanca the XIV Queen Sofia Award for Ibero-American Poetry, consisting of €42,100 for his literary career. In his acceptance speech, Gelman said: "I feel that this award is above all a recognition to poetry that is born from regional roots, a recognition to those who insist on this hard work, trying to express the center of their obsessions even knowing that there is no center but an unsheltered open sky. In their name, I receive and dedicate to those who could well be here in my place. . . . "

Lastly, in November 28, 2007, he received the most prestigious literary award in the Spanish language, the Miguel de Cervantes Prize, with a cash award of €90,400. Gelman was the fourth Argentinian to receive this award after Jorge Luis Borges, Jorge Sabato, and Adolfo Bioy Casares. After the meeting that was held by the jury, the director of Real Academia Española, Mr. Víctor García de la Concha, agreed to award Gelman the "Novel español" (Spanish Nobel Prize) because his work "enriches Spanish literature" and "he never abdicated from his primary commitment to poetry."

Gelman received the news when he received a call from the writer and Spain's former culture minister, César Antonio Molina Sánchez. Silvina Friera transcribed his first impressions in an interview in *Página/12*. "I read yesterday in the newspapers that there were some first-line candidates: Nicanor Parra, Mario Benedetti, Juan Goytisolo, Juan Marsé, José Emilio Pacheco, Blanca Varela. And when I saw the list I said to myself: Juan, you don't, it's impossible. But it was not like that. This morning I received a call from the Spain's culture ministry to let me know the jury's decision. I also received a call from Kirchner and Cristina. Néstor told me that he was proud; Cristina, when the news arrived in Paraguay, was extremely happy."

The poet thanked the jury and said: "Today poetry is awarded, as it was awarded yesterday and even before in this historic auditorium where great voices still resound. And it is something admirable in this 'Dürftiger Zeite,' these mean times, these penury times, as were qualified by Hölderlin asking himself 'Wozu Dichter,' Why poets? What would he say today, in a world where every three seconds and a half a child younger than five years old dies of incurable disease, starving, or poverty? I ask myself how many would have died since I started to say these words, but poetry is there: standing up against death."

III. Spoken-Word Albums

Gelman was also a great poetry reciter. His sensibility was not limited to the solitary exercise of poetry; he would also try the craft of interpreting his own work. He had an outstanding career of reading in public and on recordings. He had a very peculiar style. His slow pace was recognized and admired by his colleagues and the public who attended his presentations. He used different registers with different accompaniments in different countries. Among his recordings, the most internationally known are the following:

In 1965, as a permanent collaborator of Ediciones Horizonte, a small publishing company directed by Carlos Brocato and José Luis Mangieri that would later take the name La rosa blindada, Gelman and his colleagues decided to record their first LP, *Madrugada* (*Dawn*). With a first edition of five hundred copies, this album was financed with the help of some painter friends, who "donated a painting, and the profit of the sale paid for the luxury of this adventure," as Gelman mentions in an interview for *La Maga*. The album includes the music of Juan Carlos "Tata" Cedrón and the poetry of Juan Gelman, who tells how he experienced this first project: "I went often to Cedrón's house. Recorded some poems. We listened to them. He had already composed two *milongas,* without the lyrics. We started thinking about the potential of this. At first, we were using other poems. Then we realized some didn't match and others were forced. In some cases, "Extrañadura" ("Missing"), for example, Cedrón put music to a finished poem; in other cases ("Siete," "Pasaba algo") ("Seven," "Something's Going On") I did the poem myself, over the music or within it. It took us a lot of time to compose the album, about a year to get a unified style."

The year after the recording of *Madrugada*, Gelman released his second album, called *Gotán,* through Fonoeléctricos label. Two years later, in 1968, came the time for a third disc, *Cuerpo que me querés* (*Body that Loves Me*).

In 1970, with three albums already recorded, Gelman and Cedrón created a show for musical theater titled *Fábulas* (*Fables*) that was presented in the theater Planeta of Buenos Aires. In an interview published in *Brecha,* Gelman recalled the genesis of the musical project:

> Once many years ago, Tata Cedrón, who was just beginning to compose, came to me asking if he could use one of my poems for the lyrics of a *tango* he recently composed. I told him yes; that's how this collaboration started, always with the same terms: He borrows my poems and musicalizes them, except for one time that was kind of an oral writing, because I was listening to the music and putting down the words. After that, Tata widened his range. He put music to poems from Dylan Thomas, Brecht, Francisco Urondo, and others. Facing the idea of making discs and shows from that, we saw the possibility of creating a poetic climate between words and music, not necessarily with sung words but spoken. I always thought that there are very subtle threads that come together and create a climate. That's how we made the poetry show we called *Fábulas.* It was a theatrical show with dialogues and dance, waltzes and tangos.

After this success, Gelman and Cedrón decided to record together their fourth album. In 1971 *Fábulas* appeared, edited by the label La rosa blindada. The next year, Gelman recorded *Le chant du coq* (*The Song of the Rooster*) in Paris, a spoken-word disc that compiled some of his poetry, accompanied by the music of the Cuarteto Cedrón, "Paco" Ibáñez (voice and guitar), and François Rabbath on bass.

In 1973, Gelman wrote *La trampera general* (*The General Trapper*), an opera with Tata Cedrón that was never released, but was partially compiled on the disc *De Argentina* (*From Argentina*), edited by Polydor in Paris, 1973.

In the same year, his sixth album called *Chansons d'amour d'Occitanie et autres histoires / Canciones de amor de Occitania y otros casos* (*Love*

Songs from Occitania and Other Stories), was recorded in Paris in 1973 and appeared in 1975, edited by Polydor. Some of the poems, like "Los Tanguitos," "Casos," "Brunessen," and "Saufre," anonymous poems from Provence, were translated by Juan Gelman and set to music by Cedrón.

In 1978, he released in Paris his seventh album, titled *Chances suertes* (*Lucky Chances*), written in 1973, with the participation of the Cedrón quartet. The composition, which was also included in *Chances et instrumentaux* (*Chances and Instrumentals*) published by Polydor and released in France in 1976, takes the form of a cantata.

His eighth album was released through the label of La Casa de las Américas de Cuba (The House of the Americas of Cuba). The recording, titled *Juan Gelman en su propia voz* (*Juan Gelman in His Own Voice*), which included some of the author's poems, was part of the collection titled *Palabra de esta América No. 40* (*Word of this America No. 40*).

In 1994, Juan Gelman released two audio books titled *Poemas* (*Poems*) and *Ruiseñores* (*Nightingales*).

Three years later, he released two albums in Buenos Aires. The first, published under the *Página/12* label, was entitled *Eduardo Galeano, Juan Gelman.* The second, entitled *Una manu tumó l'otra,* (*One Hand Took the Other*), released under the Acqua label, included eighteen songs interpreted by singer Dina Rot. This recording, which also includes songs written by Clarisse Nicoidsky, was recorded entirely in Sephardic. Gelman published a thank-you letter in the *La Maga* of Buenos Aires to Dina Rot for what he considered to be an excellent interpretation:

> You have given a hidden dimension to the poems, and they are made real in your voice. They could also provoke other ideas: for example, that music rescues a dimension of time—of the time of that tongue—which exalts your continuity, your presence, your modernity, as they say nowadays. It's *raison d'être*, though some say it has been extinguished. You [referring to Rot and Eduardo Laguillo, the producer of the album] have returned to the present that which one assumes was past, that is to say, you have brightened its future, because the past was always the future, at some point. And that future lies dormant, it even seems to sleep. You will forever be installed in that heartbeat. And there is something

> that particularly moved me, and even to tears: The eternally trembling Jew in "Quedati cun mi" (Stay With Me) and in "Ondi sta yave your corason" (Where is the Key to Your Heart). I can see and feel here my grandfather, a Rabbi lost in the depths of Ukraine.

Gelman's thirteenth LP, titled *La voz de Juan Gelman: Poesía en la residencia* (*The Voice of Juan Gelman: Poetry in Residence*), which appeared in Madrid in 2007 under *Publicaciones de la Residencia de Estudiantes* (Publications from the Student Residence) label, was recorded during a lecture delivered by the author at the student residence.

On September 28, 2010, Gelman performed a poetry recital in Barcelona, at the Oriol Martorell Auditori in celebration of the hundred-year anniversary of *Casa Amèrica Catalunya* (House of America, Catalonia). The presentation was videotaped and published under the title *Del Amor* (*Of Love*). The presentation included poems read by Gelman and music composed and performed by bandoneonist Rodolfo Mederos, bass guitarist Sergio Rivas, and guitarist Armando De la Vega. The show also included images of the work of Argentinian painter Juan José Cambre and was hosted by the dramatist and actress Cristina Banegas.

IV. Books by Juan Gelman

Poetic Works. First Editions

1956. *Violín y otras cuestiones*. Buenos Aires: Editor Gleizer. Prologue by Raúl González Tuñón.

1959. *El juego en que andamos*. Buenos Aires: Nueva Expresión.

1961. *Velorio del solo*. Buenos Aires: Nueva Expresión.

1962. *Gotán*. Buenos Aires: Ediciones Horizonte. La rosa blindada Collection.

1965. *Cólera buey*. La Habana: La Tertulia, 1965. Consists of nine books and two thousand poems written between 1962 and 1968. He published the complete version of *Cólera buey* in Buenos Aires in 1971.

1969. *Traducciones III. Los poemas de Sidney West*. Buenos Aires: Editorial Galerna.

1971. *Fábulas*. Buenos Aires: Ediciones La rosa blindada.

1973. *Relaciones*. Buenos Aires: Ediciones La rosa blindada.

1980. *Hechos y relaciones*. Barcelona: Editorial Lumen. *Hechos* was published together with a re-release of *Relaciones* under the title *Hechos y relaciones*. This is officially his first book written in exile.

1980. *Si dulcemente*. Barcelona: Lumen. It includes *Notas*, *Carta abierta,* and *Si dulcemente*.

1982. *Hacia el sur*. México D. F.: Marcha Editores.

1982. *Citas y comentarios*. Madrid: Visor.

1985. *La junta luz: Oratorio a Las Madres de Plaza de Mayo*. Buenos Aires: Libros de Tierra Firme.

1986. *Com/posiciones*. Barcelona: Ediciones Del Mall.

1986. *Interrupciones 2*. Buenos Aires: Libros de Tierra Firme. Encompasses four books: *Bajo la lluvia ajena (notas al pie de una derrota)*, *Hacia el sur*, *Com/posiciones,* and *Eso*.

1988. *Interrupciones 1*. Buenos Aires: Libros de Tierra Firme. Includes *Hechos y relaciones*, *Notas*, *Carta abierta*, *Si dulcemente,* and *Citas y comentarios*.

1988. *Anunciaciones*. Madrid: Visor.

1989. *Carta a mi madre*. Buenos Aires: Libros de Tierra Firme. Dedicated to his son, Marcelo Ariel.

1993. *Salario del impío*. Buenos Aires: Libros de Tierra Firme.

1994. *Dibaxu*. Buenos Aires: Seix Barral.

1997. *Incompletamente*. Buenos Aires: Seix Barral.

2001. *Valer la pena*. Buenos Aires: Seix Barral. Title taken from the poem, "Cada día que pasa" ("Each Day that Passes") by Francisco "Paco" Urondo.

2004. *País que fue será*. Buenos Aires: Seix Barral.

2007. *Mundar*. Buenos Aires: Seix Barral.

2009. *De atrásalante en su porfía*. Buenos Aires: Seix Barral.

2011. *El emperrado corazón amora*. Buenos Aires: Seix Barral. This title is taken from "Sí" ("Yes"), a poem that is included in the completed version of *Cólera buey*.

2013. *Hoy*. Buenos Aires: Seix Barral.

2014. *Amaramara*. Mexico D.F.: La Otra Editorial. Temblor de cielo Collection. Twenty-nine late posthumous poems dedicated to his wife, Mara La Madrid.

Narrative Works

1974. *Perú: el poder al pueblo*. Buenos Aires: Crisis.

1997. *Prosa de prensa. Documentos*. Buenos Aires, Ediciones B. Compiling of Gelman's articles published in the newspaper *Página/12*.

1997. *Ni el flaco perdón de Dios*. Buenos Aires: Planeta. Written with Mara La Madrid.

1999. *Nueva prosa de prensa*. Buenos Aires, Editorial Vergara. Second part of the compiling of articles published in *Página/12*.

2003. *Afganistán Iraq. El imperio empantanado*. Buenos Aires: Planeta.

2005. *Miradas: de poetas, escritores y artistas*. Buenos Aires: Seix Barral.

2009. *Escritos urgentes (I)* and *Escritos urgentes (II.)* Buenos Aires: Capital intelectual. First and second parts from a compilation of articles published by Gelman.

Journalism: Magazines, Newspapers, and News Agencies

1954. *Nuestra Palabra*. Buenos Aires. German served as editor.

1954. *Xinhua (New China.)* Buenos Aires. Gelman worked as a correspondent of the *People's Republic of China's* news agency.

1954. *La Hora*. Buenos Aires. Gelman was an active contributor to the Argentine Communist Party's magazine.

1958. *Nueva Expresión*. Buenos Aires. Gelman took part in the editing and assembly of the magazine alongside Juan Carlos Portantiero, Roberto Hozni, and Andres Rivera.

1964. *La rosa blindada*. Buenos Aires. Gelman became a member of this literary group and publishing company that is directed by Carlos Brocato and José Luis Mangieri.

1966. *Confirmado*. Buenos Aires. Gelman collaborated in this magazine under the supervision of Horacio Verbitsky.

1969. *Panorama*. Buenos Aires. Gelman acted as editor-in-chief alongside Homero Alsina Thevenet, Miguel Grinberg, Daniel Muchnik, Carlos Ulanovsky, Francisco Urondo, Horacio Salas, and Edgardo Da Mommio.

1969. *Los Libros*. Buenos Aires. Gelman served as an editor and writer.

1970. *Primera Plana*. Buenos Aires. Gelman occupied the position of the editor-in-chief.

1971–1973. *La Opinión*. Buenos Aires. He served as editor in chief and director of the cultural supplement of the newspaper led then by Jacobo Timerman. Gelman collaborated with, among others, Tomás Eloy Martínez, Francisco Urondo, José María Pasquini Durán, Osvaldo Soriano, Rodolfo Walsh, Horacio Verbitsky, Miguel Bonasso, Nicolás Casullo, and Hermenegildo Sábat.

1973–1975. *Crisis*. Buenos Aires. Gelman served as editor in chief. The magazine, founded by the sponsor Federico Vogelius, soon became a transcendent magazine both in the local and the international panorama, having around fifty thousand issues printed. Among other collaborations, the most meaningful were those from Eduardo Galeano, Mario Benedetti, Vicente Zito Lema, and Aníbal Ford. Gelman walked away in the middle of 1975 after working on twenty successive issues because of the constant threats from the Triple A (Alianza Anticomunista Argentina [Argentine Anticommunist Alliance]).

1974. *Noticias*. Buenos Aires. He served as editor in chief. The publication belonged to the organization Montoneros. The collaborators were, among others, Francisco Urondo, Horacio Verbitsky, Rodolfo Walsh, and Miguel Bonasso.

1975. *Inter Press Service*. Rome. Exiled in Rome, Gelman began working in this news agency where he was in charge of the network of Latin American correspondents.

1979. *Nueva Nicaragua*. Managua. With the triumph of the Nicaraguan revolution, Gelman collaborated with the Sandinistas' news agency.

1987. *Página/12*. Buenos Aires. Gelman collaborated with the newspaper until his last days.

2005. *Milenio*. Mexico. Gelman collaborated regularly until his death.

2005. *Prensa Latina*. Gelman participated in this Informative Latin American agency based in Cuba.

2008. *Cuadernos Hispanoamericanos*. Madrid. The magazine, which focused on literature in Spanish published worldwide, published many of Gelman's articles.

V. The Essential Juan Gelman: Anthologies

1960. *Poemas*. La Habana: Casa de las Américas. Compiled by Mario Benedetti and Jorge Timossi.

1963. *Traigo una voz encarcelada.* Buenos Aires: Movimiento por la Legalidad Democrática.

1968. *Poemas.* La Habana: Casa de las Américas.

1975. *Obra poética.* Buenos Aires: Ediciones Corregidor.

1984. *Exilio.* Buenos Aires: Ediciones Legasa. It contains three texts by Osvaldo Bayer and the poems of *Bajo la lluvia ajena* (*notas al pie de una derrota*).

1985. *Poesía.* La Habana: Casa de las Américas. Preface and selection by Víctor Casaus.

1993. *Antología poética.* Montevideo: Vintén. Selection, preface, and bibliography by Lilián Uribe.

1993. *Antología personal.* Buenos Aires: Desde la gente.

1993. *En abierta oscuridad.* México: Siglo XXI. It includes drawings by Luciano SpaNo.

1994. *De palabra: Poesía III (1973-1989).* Madrid: Visor. Preface by Julio Cortázar.

1994. *Antología poética.* Buenos Aires: Espasa Calpe. Selection and preface by Jorge Fondebrider.

1997. *Debí decir te amo. Antología personal.* Buenos Aires: Planeta.

1998. *Antología poética.* Buenos Aires: Fondo Nacional de las Artes.

1999. *En abierta oscuridad.* México, D.F.: Siglo Veintiuno Editores.

1999. *53 poemas.* Buenos Aires: Grupo Editorial Grijalbo Mondadori. Selection by Sebastián Robles.

2000. *En el hoy y mañana y ayer.* México, D.F.: Universidad Nacional Autónoma de México.

2000. *Tantear la noche.* Lanzarote: Fundación César Manrique. It includes twenty-two unpublished poems by Juan Gelman.

2001. *Pesar todo: antología.* Cuba: Fondo Editorial Casa de las Américas.

2003. *Huellas en el agua = Spuren im Wasser.* Zürich: Teamart. Translation by Tobias Burghardt.

2005. *Sombra de vuelta y de ida.* México, D.F.: Taller Ditoria. Ideogram by R. Turnbull.

2005. *Oficio Ardiente.* Madrid: Patrimonio Nacional. Edition and introduction by Maria Ángeles Pérez López. Selection by Maria Ángeles Pérez López and Juan Gelman. Preface by Julio Cortázar.

2006. *Doveri dell'esilio.* Novara, Italia: Edición numerada de Interlinea. Translation by L. Branchini.

2007. *Fulgor del aire.* Santiago del Chile: Lom Ediciones.

2008. *Otromundo: Antología 1956-2007.* Madrid: Fondo de Cultura Económica. Universidad de Alcalá de Henares. Selection by Eduardo Hurtado. Preface by Carlos Monsiváis.
2008. *De palabra: Poesía III (1973-1989).* Madrid: Visor Libros.
2008. *Tiempo.* Madrid: Endymion, 2008.
2011. *El ciempiés y la araña.* México: Capital intelectual. Drawings by Eleonora Arroyo.
2012. *Poesía reunida.* Buenos Aires: Seix Barral.

VI. Juan Gelman in Theory

1964. Bullrich, Santiago. *Recreación y realidad en Pisarello, Gelman y Vallejo.* Buenos Aires: Jorge Álvarez.
1971. Benedetti, Mario. "Juan Gelman y su ardua empresa de matar la melancolía." *Los poetas comunicantes*, 1971: 55–82.
1972. Barros, Daniel. *Poesía sudamericana actual (Gelman, Teillier, Benedetti).* Madrid: Miguel Castellote.
1980. O'Hara, Edgar. "Juan Gelman: la realidad contra la poesía." *Desde Melibea.* Lima: Ediciones Ruray.
1985. Achugar, Hugo. "La poesía de Juan Gelman o la ternura desatada." *Hispanoamérica: Revista de Literatura* (41), 1985: 95–102.
1985. Sheerer, Thomas M. *La sangre y el papel: eine Vorstudie zur Lyrik des Argentiniers Juan Gelman.* Augsburg: Institut für Spanien und Lateinamerikastudien, U Augsburg.
1987. Giordano, Jaime. "Juan Gelman: el dolor de los otros." *Dioses, antidioses/ Ensayos críticos sobre poesía hispanoamericana.* Santiago: Ediciones Lar.
1988. Mero, Roberto. *Conversaciones con Juan Gelman. Contraderrota, Montoneros y la revolución perdida.* Buenos Aires: Contrapunto.
1989. Caisso, Claudia y Peschiera, Luis. "Gelman: cita y comentarios con que apaciguar la extrañeza." *Cuadernos de la Comuna* 18, 1989: 33–69.
1990. Benedetti, Mario. "Gelman hace delirar a las palabras." *La realidad y la palabra.* Barcelona: Destino, 1990: 49–70.
1990. Dalmaroni, Miguel. "Inestabilidad y reconformación del sujeto en los primeros textos de Juan Gelman." *Estudios de lírica*

contemporánea. La Plata: Facultad de Humanidades y Ciencias de la Educación, Universidad de La Plata, 1990: 67–89.
1990. Rama, Ángel. "Juan Gelman, la poesía en tiempo de los asesinos." *Revista La Maga*. Buenos Aires: Maga Ediciones, 1990: 66–71.
1992. Porrúa, Ana María. "Relaciones de Juan Gelman. El cuestionamiento de las certezas poéticas." *Revista de crítica literaria latinoamericana* 35, 1992: 120–150.
1992. Santos Sáez, Carlos y Rimondino, Adrián. "Juan Gelman, el poeta más grande de la Argentina." *Revista Lea* 19.2, 1992: 148–188.
1993. Dalmaroni, Miguel. *Juan Gelman contra las fabulaciones del mundo*. Buenos Aires: Almagesto.
1994. Boccanera, Jorge. *Confiar en el misterio (Viaje por la poesía de Juan Gelman)*. Buenos Aires: Sudamericana.
1995. Críticos varios. *Como temblor del aire/ La poesía de Juan Gelman* (compilation of articles by Lilián Uribe). Montevideo: Vintén.
1996. Freidemberg, Daniel. "Poesía contra poema. La estrategia del inacabamiento en Juan Gelman." *Atípicos en la literatura latinoamericana*. Buenos Aires: Eudeba, 1996: 109–130.
1996. Sillato, María del Carmen. "Las estrategias de la otredad en la poesía de Juan Gelman." Diss., U. of Toronto.
1996. Sillato, María del Carmen. *Juan Gelman. Las estrategias de la otredad. Heteronimia. Intertextualidad. Traducción*. Buenos Aires: Beatriz Viterbo Editora.
1996. Portilla, Enrique. "Las circunstancias del corazón. Entrevista con Juan Gelman." *La Jornada Semanal*. México, 1996.
1997. Crites, Elsa. "Poetry versus Dictatorship in Argentina during Proceso: Juan Gelman and Juan González." Diss., Florida State University.
1997. Freidemberg, Daniel. "La poesía de Gelman: cuando surgen las palabras." *El País Cultural*. Madrid, 17 October 1997: 415.
1997. Appratto, Roberto. "El diálogo con el lector." *El País Cultural*. Madrid, n. 415, 17 October 1997.
1998. Montanaro, Pablo y Ture (Rubén Salvador). *Palabra de Gelman*. Buenos Aires: Corregidor.
1999. Victoria Suárez, María. "Cuando un poema es más efectivo que una bala: Incompletamente de Juan Gelman." *La Nación (La Bitácora de Gelman)*. Buenos Aires.
1999. Galeano, Eduardo. "El poeta que busca y espera." *Página/12*. Buenos Aires, 14 November 1999.

2000. Sillato, María del Carmen. "Dibaxu de Juan Gelman: la poesía desde las 'exiliadas raíces de la lengua'." *Actas del XII Congreso Internacional de Hispanistas*, 2000: 137–181.

2000. Tamargo Cordero, Elena. *Juan Gelman: poesía de la sombra de la memoria*. México: Universidad Iberoamericana.

2000. Bru, José. *Acercamiento a Juan Gelman*. México: Universidad de Guadalajara, Departamento de Estudios Literarios.

2000. Correa Mujica, Miguel. "Juan Gelman y la nueva poesía hispanoamericana." *Espéculo. Revista de estudios literarios 18. (Universidad Complutense de Madrid)*. 2000: 16–34.

2001. Correa Mujica, Miguel. "Juan Gelman y la nueva poesía hispanoamericana." *Espéculo, revista de estudios literarios*. Madrid, n. 18, July–October 2001.

2001. Rojo, José Andrés. "Juan Gelman, poeta: 'Todo mi dolor ha pasado a la literatura'." *El País*. Guadalajara, 4 December 2001.

2001. Zeiger, Claudio. "El oficio de poeta." *Radar. Página/12*. Buenos Aires, October 2001.

2002. Gómez Mango, Edmundo. *La poésie de Juan Gelman et l'appel des disparus*. Paris: Myriam Solal.

2004. "Juan Gelman: 'El dolor no es la fuente de inspiración'." *El Mundo* 27 September 2007.

2004. Gómez Mango, Edmundo. *El llamado de los desaparecidos: sobre la poesía de Juan Gelman*. Montevideo: Cal y Canto.

2004. Varela de Rozas, Beatriz. "Juan Gelman, poeta argentiNo." *Literatura perseguida*. México, 1 November 2004.

2005. Fabry, Geneviève. "La escritura del duelo en la poesía de Juan Gelman." *Anuario de Estudios Filológicos* XXVIII, 2005: 55–69.

2005. Pérez López, Maria Ángeles. *Juan Gelman: poesía y coraje*. Santa Cruz de Tenerife: La Página.

2006. Montanaro, Pablo. *Juan Gelman. Esperanza, utopía y resistencia*. Buenos Aires: Ediciones Lea.

2006. Viau, Susana (entrevista a Juan Gelman). "Llegué a los 75 sin darme cuenta." *Página/12* 24 March 2006.

2007. Muleiro, Vicente (entrevista a Juan Gelman). "'Intento dar existencia al futuro y, por lo tanto, también al presente'. El reconocido poeta argentino publica 'Mundar'." *Clarín* 30 September 2007.

2007. Campos, Marco Antonio. "Juan Gelman: poesía con pájaros." *La Jornada Semanal*. México, n. 661, 4 November 2007.

2007. Fernández-Aceytuno, Mónica. "Gelman." *ABC*. Madrid, 1 February 2007.
2007. "Juan Gelman." *El País*. Madrid, 5 May 2007.
2008. Fabry, Geneviève. *Las formas del vacío. La escritura del duelo en la poesía de Juan Gelman*. Amsterdam-New York: Rodopi.
2008. *El Emperrado corazón amora: homenaje a Juan Gelman, Premio Cervantes 2007 (del 23 abril al 22 junio de 2008)*. Madrid: Museo Luis González Robles; Universidad de Alcalá de Henares. Alcalá de Henares.
2008. "Gelman: En un lugar de La Mancha." *El País*. Madrid, 23 April 2008.
2008. "Gelman arremete contra el olvido. El poeta argentino recuerda la dictadura de su país en el discurso del Cervantes." *El País*. Madrid, 24 April 2008.
2008. "Gelman se solidarizó con Cardenal." *La Nación*. Buenos Aires, 10 September 2008.
2008. Job Valle, Vanessa. "Juan Gelman abrió en el Círculo la lectura continuada del Quijote." *ABC*. Madrid, 24 April 2008.
2008. "Juan Gelman deposita su legado para la posteridad en Madrid." *ABC*. Madrid, 25 April 2008.
2008. Luján Atienza, Ángel. "Summa Gelman." *Revista de Libros*, No.141, 2008, page 41.
2008. "La poesía puede cambiar a los seres humanos. Juan Gelman en Costa Rica." *Red Cultura*. Costa Rica, 25 May 2008.
2011. Prieto de Paula, Ángel L. "Las ruinas de la tarde." *El País, Babelia*. Madrid, 7 May 2011, page 9.

VII. Translations of Juan Gelman's Literary Work

1978. *So arbeitet die Hoffnung: Lyrik des aregntinischen Widerstandes*. Übertragung und Nachwort von Wolfgang Heuer und Miquel Salí; mit einem Geleitwort von Eduardo GaleaNo. Berlin: Oberbaumverlag, 1978.
1981. *Silence des yeux: poèmes*. Paris: Éditions du Cerf, 1981. Translation into French of *Relaciones*, *Hechos,* and *Notas*, with a prologue by Julio Cortázar.

1989. *Bein og bebudelser: diki i utvalg.* Oslo: Gyldenal

1997. *Unthinkable Tenderness.* Berkeley: University of California Press. Selection and translation by Joan Lindgren, with a foreword by Eduardo GaleaNo.

1997. *Juan Gelman: Obscur Ouvert.* Luxemburgo-Québec: Editions PhiEcrits des Forges. Selection and translation by Jean Portante.

1997. *Les poèmes de Sidney West.* Grâne: Créaphis.

2000. *Treffpunkt: fast vergessenes Frangment eines Gesprächs mit dem argentinischen Dichter Juan Gelman im Jahre 1987.* Augsburg: Knape.

2000. *Dibaxu=Debajo=Darunter.* Juan Gelman; aus dem Sephardischen ins Spanische von Juan Gelman; aus dem Sephardischen und Spanischen von Tobias Burghardt. Dürnau (Deutschland): Edition 350 im Verlag der Kooperative Dürnau.

2001. *Die letzen Splitter des Lichts: Gedichte = Las últimas astillas del reflejo / Olga Orozco, Alejandra Pizarnik, Juan Gelman.* Zürich: Teamart-Verlag.

2003. *Huellas en el agua = Spuren im Wasser.* Zürich: Teamart. Ausgewählt, eingeführt und dem argentinischen Spanisch von Juana & Tobias Burghardt.

VIII. Bibliography

"Cronología bio-bibliografía de Juan Gelman." *La Maga.* No. 28. Buenos Aires, 1 July 1997.

"El destierro." *La Maga.* No. 28.

"El pibe Juan." *La Maga.* No. 28.

"Gelman: En un lugar de La Mancha." *El País.* Madrid, 23 April 2008.

"Juan el porteño." *La Maga.* No. 28.

"Juan Gelman: 'El dolor no es la fuente de inspiración'." *El Mundo*, 27 September 2007.

"Juan política y exilio." *La Maga.* No. 28.

"Juan y los discos." *La Maga.* No. 28.

Adorno, Theodor. *Crítica cultural y sociedad.* Madrid: Colección: Los grandes pensadores, Sarpe, 1984.

Adorno, Theodor. "La educación después de Auschwitz." *Consignas.* Buenos Aires: Amorrortu, 1993.

Barros, Daniel. *Poesía sudamericana actual (Gelman, Teillier, Benedetti).* Madrid: Miguel Castellote, 1972.

Bloom, Harold. *El canon occidental.* Barcelona: Anagrama, 1995.

Bloom, Harold. *La angustia de las influencias.* Caracas: Monte Ávila Editores, 1991.

Boccanera, Jorge. *Confiar en el misterio. Viaje por la poesía de Juan Gelman.* Buenos Aires: Editorial Sudamericana, 1994.

Bru, José. *Acercamiento a Juan Gelman.* México: Universidad de Guadalajara, Departamento de Estudios Literarios, 2000.

Bullrich, Santiago. *Recreación y realidad en Pisarello, Gelman y Vallejo.* Buenos Aires: Jorge Álvarez, 1964.

Campos, Marco Antonio. "Gelman por Campos." *La Otra. Revista de Poesía.* Abril 2010.

Cella, Susana. "Magia fantasma niebla poesía." *Radar. Página/12.* Buenos Aires, 19 January 2014.

Claudel, Paul. *Réflexion sur la poésie.* Paris: Gallimard, 1963.

Crites, Elsa. "Poetry versus Dictatorship in Argentina during Proceso: Juan Gelman and Juan González." Diss., Florida State University, 1997.

Dalmaroni, Miguel. *Juan Gelman contra las fabulaciones del mundo.* Buenos Aires: Almagesto. Colección Perfiles, 1993.

Elías, Jorge. *Maten al cartero: posdata del asedio a la prensa durante las dictaduras militares del Cono Sur.* Buenos Aires: Fundación Cadal, 2005.

Esquivada, Gabriela. *Noticias de los Montoneros. La historia del diario que no pudo anunciar la revolución.* Buenos Aires: Editorial Sudamericana, 2005.

Fabry, Geneviève. *Las formas del vacío. La escritura del duelo en la poesía de Juan Gelman.* New York: Editions Rodopi B. V., 2008.

Gómez Mango, Edmundo. *La poésie de Juan Gelman et l'appel des disparus.* Paris: Myriam Solal, 2002.

Fontanet, Hernán. *Al sur de casi todo. Humberto Costantini y su obra.* Buenos Aires, Argentina: Universidad Pedagógica Provincial, 2017.

Fontanet, Hernán. *Fervor y exilio en la poética de Humberto Costantini.* New York: The Edwin Mellen Press, 2008.

Fontanet, Hernán. *Francisco Urondo y su poesía, un arma cargada de futuro.* Newark, DE: Juan de la Cuesta - Hispanic Monographs, 2012.

Fontanet, Hernán. *Gelman. Un poeta y su vida.* Buenos Aires, Argentina: Editorial Aguilar, 2015.

Fontanet, Hernán. *In Praise of Tears: The Quest for Identity in Humberto Costantini's Poetry.* Porto Alegre, Brazil: Editoria da Pontifícia Universidade Católica do Rio Grande do Sul, 2016.

Fontanet, Hernán. *Juan Gelman y su tiempo: Historias, poemas y reflexiones.* Barcelona, Spain: Editorial Alrevés, 2015.

Fontanet, Hernán. *Modelo y subversión en la poética de Leónidas Lamborghini.* New York: The Edwin Mellen Press, 2009.

Fontanet, Hernán. *Poéticas de exilio.* Madrid, Spain: Universidad Autónoma de Madrid. Rebelion.org Libros Libres, 2004.

Fontanet, Hernán. *The Unfinished Song of Francisco Urondo: When Poetry is Not Enough.* Lanham, MD: University Press of America, 2014.

Freidemberg, Daniel. "Libro por libro." *La Maga.* No. 28.

Kohut, David R., Vilella, Olga y Julian, Beatrice. *Historical Dictionary of the Dirty Wars.* Lanham, MD: Scarecrow Press, 2003.

Mero, Roberto. *Conversaciones con Juan Gelman.* Buenos Aires: Contrapunto, 1987.

Montanaro, Pablo. *Juan Gelman. Esperanza, utopía y resistencia.* Buenos Aires: Ediciones Lea, 2006.

Muleiro, Vicente y Pogoriles, Eduardo. "Ningún elogio o premio escribe por vos." *Revista Ñ.* Buenos Aires, 11 March 2006.

Pérez López, María Ángeles. *Juan Gelman: poesía y coraje.* Santa Cruz de Tenerife: La Página, 2005.

Riechmann, Jorge. "Lumbre Libertad (para Juan Gelman.)" *Resistencia de materiales. Ensayos sobre el mundo y la poesía y el mundo 1988-2004.* Barcelona: Montesinos, 2006.

Saccomanno, Guillermo. "Cuestiones con Gelman." *Radar. Página/12.* Buenos Aires, 19 January 2014.

Sasturain, Juan. "Poeta en el costado izquierdo." *Radar. Página/12.* Buenos Aires, 19 January 2014.

Sheerer, Thomas M. *La sangre y el papel: eine Vorstudie zur Lyrik des Argentiniers Juan Gelman.* Augsburg: Institut für Spanien und Lateinamerikastudien, U Augsburg, 1985.

Sillato, María del Carmen. *Juan Gelman. Las estrategias de la otredad. Heteronimia. Intertextualidad. Traducción.* Buenos Aires: Beatriz Viterbo Editora, 1996.

Tamargo Cordero, Elena. *Juan Gelman: poesía de la sombra de la*

memoria. México: Universidad Iberoamericana, 2000.
Uribe, Lilián. *Como temblor del aire: la poesía de Juan Gelman*. Ensayos críticos. Montevideo: Vinten Editor, 1995.
Vallejo, César. "Idilio muerto." *Los heraldos negros*. Barcelona: Red Ediciones, 2011.
Vallejo, César. "Viniere el malo, con un trono al hombro…." *Poemas Humanos. Obra Poética Completa*. Madrid: Alianza, 2000.
Verbitsky, Horacio. "Del amor y la guerra." *Página/12*. Buenos Aires, 27 April 2008.
Verbitsky, Horacio. "El universo desnudo." *Página/12*. Buenos Aires, 3 February 2014.
Verduchi, Enzia. "El oficio ardiente." *Brecha*. Montevideo, 19 June 2004.
Viau, Susana. "Me distraje. Llegué a los 75 sin darme cuenta." *Página/12*. Buenos Aires, 10 March 2006.
Viñas, David. *Literatura argentina y realidad política, de Sarmiento a Cortázar*. Buenos Aires: Ediciones Siglo Veinte, 1971.
Yurkiévich, Saúl. "La violencia estremecedora de lo real." *Río de la Plata*. No. 7. París, 1988.

Notes

1. Eduardo Galeano, "Los Nadies," *El libro de los abrazos*, Ediciones de la cueva, 1989, 52: "Los nadies, que cuestan menos que la bala que los mata."
2. Outcomes of this sort occurred when Gelman and many other unsatisfied intellectuals were forced into exile or were assassinated.
3. Montoneros was one of the most powerful guerrilla organizations of Latin America at that time. As an armed wing of the Argentine Peronist movement, it was characterized by violent urban terrorist actions that included political kidnappings and assassinations.
4. José Emilio Pacheco, "Adiós a Juan Gelman," *Página/12* (Buenos Aires, February 11, 2014).
5. Rodolfo Braceli, "Juan Gelman: 'El único consuelo es que el tiempo envejece con uno," *La Nación* (Buenos Aires, January 14, 2014).
6. "El pibe Juan," *La Maga*, No. 28. (Buenos Aires, July 1, 1997).
7. "El pibe Juan," *La Maga*, No. 28.
8. "El pibe Juan," *La Maga*, No. 28.
9. "Me batían 'el pibe taquito,'" *Revista Veintitrés*, No. 170 (Buenos Aires, October 10, 2001), 73. Interview by Miguel Russo; also published in Sololiteratura.com under the title "Juan Gelman: el gran poeta en primera persona."
10. Rodolfo Braceli, "Juan Gelman: 'El único consuelo es que el tiempo envejece con uno,'" *La Nación* (Buenos Aires, January 14, 2014).
11. "Me batían 'el pibe taquito,'" *Revista Veintitrés* No. 170 (Buenos Aires, October 10, 2001), 73. Interview by Miguel Russo; also published in

Sololiteratura.com under the title, "Juan Gelman: el gran poeta en primera persona."

12. Juan Gelman, "El extranjero," *Cólera buey. Poesía reunida. Tomo I* (Buenos Aires: Seix Barral 2012), 219.
13. Rodolfo Braceli, "Juan Gelman: 'El único consuelo es que el tiempo envejece con uno," *La Nación* (Buenos Aires, January 14, 2014).
14. "El pibe Juan," *La Maga*, No. 28.
15. "El pibe Juan," *La Maga*, No. 28.
16. Nayra Pérez Hernández, "El eco de la memoria: Juan Gelman y Dibaxu," *Alpha*, No. 28, Universidad de Las Palmas de Gran Canaria, Facultad de Filología Española, Clásica y Árabe (Canary Island, Spain, July 2009), 209-221.
17. "El pibe Juan," *La Maga*, No. 28.
18. Juan Gelman, *Salario del impío / Carta a mi madre* (Buenos Aires: Editorial La Página, 2011), 81.
19. *Carta a mi madre* (Monte Carmelo, Mexico, 2007), epilogue; Marco Antonio Campos, "Gelman por Campos," *La Otra. Revista de Poesía* (April 2010).
20. Juan Gelman, *Salario del impío/Carta a mi madre* (Buenos Aires: Editorial La Página, 2011), 81.
21. Juan Gelman, *Salario del impío/Carta a mi madre*, 82.
22. Juan Gelman, *Salario del impío/Carta a mi madre*, 81.
23. Juan Gelman, *Salario del impío/Carta a mi madre*, 85.
24. "Me batían 'el pibe taquito,'" *Revista Veintitrés* No. 170.
25. "El pibe Juan," *La Maga.* No. 28.
26. "El pibe Juan," *La Maga*, No. 28.
27. Interviewed by Enzia Verduchi, "El oficio ardiente," *Brecha* (Montevideo, June 19, 2004).
28. Argentine poet Pedro Bonifacio Palacios, better known by his nickname, Almafuerte, was born on May 13, 1854, and died on February 28, 1917.
29. Peronist writer Leopoldo Marechal (June 11, 1900 – June 26, 1970) was one of the most important Argentine writers of the twentieth century.
30. "Me batían 'el pibe taquito,'" *Revista Veintitrés*, No. 170.
31. "El pibe Juan," *La Maga,* No. 28.
32. Juan Gelman, "La hija," *El juego en que andamos. Poesía reunida. Tomo I* (Buenos Aires: Seix Barral, 2012), 57.
33. Juan Gelman, "Poemas con el hijo," *El juego en que andamos. Poesía reunida. Tomo I* (Buenos Aires: Seix Barral, 2012), 51.

34. Interview with Verónica Chiaravalli, "Heridas y medallas de un poeta," *La Nación* (Buenos Aires, December 10, 1997).
35. Interview with Verónica Chiaravalli, "Heridas y medallas de un poeta."
36. Places where the tango is danced.
37. "Me batían 'el pibe taquito,'" *Revista Veintitrés*, No. 170.
38. Interview with Verónica Chiaravalli, "Heridas y medallas de un poeta."
39. "Me batían 'el pibe taquito,'" *Revista Veintitrés*, No. 170.
40. Norberto Galasso, *Vida de Scalabrini Ortiz* (Buenos Aires: Ediciones Colihue, 2008), 341.
41. The Communist Party.
42. "Me batían 'el pibe taquito,'" *Revista Veintitrés*, No. 170.
43. Juan Gelman, "Oración de un desocupado," *Violín y otras cuestiones. Poesía reunida. Tomo I* (Buenos Aires: Seix Barral, 2012), 26.
44. Juan Gelman, "Niños: Corea 1952," *Violín y otras cuestiones. Poesía reunida. Tomo I*, 26.
45. Juan Gelman, "Testamento de Pepe Díaz, soldado," *El juego en que andamos. Poesía reunida. Tomo I*, 46.
46. Juan Gelman, "María la sirvienta," *El juego en que andamos. Velorio del solo. Gotán* (Buenos Aires: Editorial La Página, 2011), 87.
47. Juan Gelman, "Los amigos, *"Cólera buey. Poesía reunida. Tomo I* (Buenos Aires: Seix Barral, 2012), 177.
48. Juan Gelman, "Pensamiento," *Cólera buey* (Buenos Aires: Seix Barral), 1971.
49. On February 14, 1973, Urondo was arrested in Tortuguitas, province of Buenos Aires, with his *compañera* "Lili" Mazzaferro, his daughter Claudia, and her husband, Mario Lorenzo Koncurat, known as "El Jote." During the operation, they was also detained a few hours later with Juan Julio Roqué—leader of the Revolutionary Armed Forces—and other *compañeros* of the Montoneros organization. While this was happening, Urondo's house in Buenos Aires was leveled out—as Urondo denounced in his poem "Quiero denunciar" ("I Want to Denounce")—and his ex-wife, Graciela "Chela" Murúa, was also detained. During his arrest, Urondo wrote an emblematic poem about the unrealistic bar that deprived him of his liberty: *"Del otro lado de la reja está la realidad, de/ este lado de la reja también está/ la realidad; la única irreal/ es la reja/ La única aparente/ es la reja cuadriculando el cielo..."* (Reality is on the other side of the bar/ reality/ is also on this side of the bar/ the only thing unrealistic/ is the bar/ The only apparent thing/ is the bar gridding the sky...) Juan Gelman's "Reconocimientos" ("Recognitions") follows a certain form of

some images from Urondo's poem: *"por los barrotes de la ventanita del camión celular/ la tarde se corta en dos..."* (by the iron bars of the small window of the police truck/ the afternoon splits in two….)

50. Juan Gelman, "Situaciones," *Interrupciones 1* (Buenos Aires: Editorial La Página, 2011), 23.
51. Ángel Rama, "Juan Gelman, la poesía en el tiempo de los asesinos," *La Maga.* No. 28, 10.
52. Interview with Verónica Chiaravalli, "Heridas y medallas de un poeta," *La Nación* (Buenos Aires, December 10, 1997).
53. Beatriz Urondo and Germán Amato, *Hermano, Paco Urondo* (Buenos Aires: Nuestra América, 2007).
54. Mario Firmenich was one of the founders of the Montoneros' organization and its most important leader.
55. Interview with Verónica Chiaravalli, "Heridas y medallas de un poeta."
56. Juan Gelman, *Bajo la lluvia ajena (notas al pie de una derrota). Interrupciones 2* (Buenos Aires: Editorial La Página, 2011), 28.
57. These names allude to poets Francisco "Paco" Urondo and Dardo Dorronsoro, writers Rodolfo Walsh and Haroldo Conti, and social activists such as Mario "Jote" Lorenzo Koncurat.
58. The increase in foreign debt, the aimless open economy, and the abolition of labor rights brought a short period of economic prosperity, which was defined by the phrase "plata dulce" (easy money). This produced a great blow to the national industry and led a large part of the population to poverty.
59. With the increase of insecurity and political assassinations, the phrase "por algo será" (there must be a reason; that is, there must be a reason *that things are as they are*) was used to justify atrocities and disconnect speakers from their political responsibilities.
60. Rodolfo Galimberti was one of the most important of the Montoneros leaders.
61. *Revista Veintitrés,* No. 170 (Buenos Aires, October 10, 2001), 73. This extract is also published in *Sololiteratura.com* with the title "Juan Gelman: el gran poeta en primera persona."
62. Horacio Verbitsky. "El universo desnudo," *Página/12.* Buenos Aires, February 3, 2014.
63. Juan Gelman, "Nota VI," *Notas. Interrupciones 1.* Buenos Aires: Editorial La Página, 2011, 102.
64. Juan Gelman, "Nota XIII," *Notas. Interrupciones 1*, 111.
65. Gelman, "Nota XV," *Notas. Interrupciones 1*, 113.

66. Gelman. “Nota VII,” *Notas. Interrupciones 1*, 103.
67. Gelman, “Nota IV,” *Notas. Interrupciones 1*, 100.
68. Gelman, “Nota XI,” *Notas. Interrupciones 1*, 108.
69. Gelman, “Nota VII,” 103.
70. Gelman, “Nota IX,” *Notas. Interrupciones 1*, 106.
71. Gelman, “Nota I,” *Notas. Interrupciones 1*, 97.
72. Juan Gelman, “Nota V,” *Notas. Interrupciones 1*, 101.
73. Gelman, “Nota XIII,” 111.
74. José María Contursi (October 31, 1911 - May 11, 1972) was an Argentine tango lyricist.
75. Dardo Scavino, “Juan Gelman: la revolución es un fuego eterno,” *Les armes et les lettres*. La violence politique dans la culture du Rio de la Plata des années 1960 à nos jours. Bordeaux: Ameriber, Université de Bordeaux, 2010, 262.
76. *La Maga, No. 28.*
77. *La Maga,* No. 28.
78. *La Maga,* No. 28.
79. *La Maga,* No. 28.
80. Paul Illie, *Literatura y exilio interior: (Escritores y sociedad en la España franquista).* Madrid: Fundamentos, 1981, 39.
81. Juan Gelman, “Ausencias,” *Hechos. Interrupciones 1*, Buenos Aires: Editorial La Página, 2011, 83.
82. Gelman, “Muertes,” *Hechos. Interrupciones 1*, 77.
83. Gelman, “Descansos,” *Hechos. Interrupciones 1*, 81.
84. Juan Gelman, “Cita XXXIII (santa teresa),” *Citas. Interrupciones 1*, Buenos Aires: Editorial La Página, 2011, 287.
85. Gelman, “Cita XVII (santa teresa),” *Citas. Interrupciones 1*, 271.
86. Gelman, “Cita XLIII (santa teresa),” *Citas. Interrupciones 1*, 297.
87. Gelman, “Cita XXXVII (santa teresa),” *Citas. Interrupciones 1*, 291.
88. Gelman, “Cita V (santa teresa),” *Citas. Interrupciones 1*, 259.
89. Gelman, “Nota II,” *Notas. Interrupciones 1*, 98.
90. Gelman, “Nota XVI,” *Notas. Interrupciones 1*, 114.
91. Gelman, “Nota III,” *Notas. Interrupciones 1*, 99.
92. The play on words alludes to the German poet Hans Arp, one of the founders of Dadaism. Juan Gelman, “Homenajes,” *Hacia el sur. Interrupciones 2.* Buenos Aires: Editorial La Página, 2011, 41.
93. Gelman, “Homenajes,” 42.
94. Juan Gelman, “Aromas,” *Hacia el sur. Interrupciones 2*, 62.

95. Gelman, "Homenajes," 41.
96. Gelman, "Actos," *Hacia el sur. Interrupciones 2*, 49.
97. Gelman, "La mesa," *Hacia el sur. Interrupciones 2*, 46.
98. Juan Gelman, "la casa de la esquina ya no es un río ni llora," *Anunciaciones. Poesía reunida. Tomo II*. Buenos Aires: Seix Barral, 2012, 127.
99. Gelman, "al día vieron caras derramadas en tu perra," *Anunciaciones. Poesía reunida. Tomo II*, 135.
100. Juan Gelman, "Preposiciones," *Relaciones*. Buenos Aires: Ediciones La rosa blindada, 1973.
101. Gelman, "Relaciones," *Relaciones*.
102. Gelman, "Descansos," 81.
103. Juan Gelman, "X," *Bajo la lluvia ajena (notas al pie de un derrota). Interrupciones 2*. Buenos Aires: Editorial La Página, 2011, 19.
104. Gelman, "XV," *Bajo la lluvia ajena (notas al pie de un derrota). Interrupciones 2*, 24.
105. Gelman, "XV," 24.
106. Gelman, "XXV," *Bajo la lluvia ajena (notas al pie de un derrota). Interrupciones 2*, 36.
107. Gelman, "XIX," *Bajo la lluvia ajena (notas al pie de un derrota). Interrupciones 2*, 29.
108. "Me batían 'el pibe taquito,'" *Revista Veintitrés*, No. 170.
109. Juan Gelman. "Los ilusos," *Eso. Interrupciones 2*. Buenos Aires: Editorial La Página, 2011, 245.
110. Geneviève Fabry, *Las formas del vacío: La escritura del duelo en la poesía de Juan Gelman*. New York: Editions Rodopi B. V., 2008, 244.
111. The neologism *mares* may refer to his wife, Mara La Madrid.
112. Juan Gelman, "cuando hacés huelga de desastres caídos," *Anunciaciones. Poesía reunida. Tomo II*. Buenos Aires: Seix Barral, 2012, 151.
113. Gelman, "el canario autorizado por el comité central," *Anunciaciones. Poesía reunida. Tomo II*.
114. Gelman, "el canario autorizado por el comité central."
115. "El destierro," *La Maga*. No. 28.
116. "Me batían 'el pibe taquito,'" *Revista Veintitrés*, No. 170.
117. "El destierro," *La Maga*. No. 28.
118. Interview by Verónica Chiaravalli. *La Nación*. Buenos Aires, December 7, 1997, 1–2.
119. Juan Gelman, "Insistencias," *De atrásalante en su porfía*, 103.
120. Gelman, "Descansos," *De atrásalante en su porfía*, 121.

121. Gelman, "Intimidades," *De atrásalante en su porfía*, 127.
122. Gelman, "Huellas," *De atrásalante en su porfía*, 145.
123. Gelman, "Compañías," *De atrásalante en su porfía*, 160.
124. Gelman, "El ojo," *De atrásalante en su porfía*, 55.
125. Gelman, "Lluvia," *De atrásalante en su porfía*, 15.
126. Gelman, "O nada bueno," *De atrásalante en su porfía*, 144.
127. Gelman, "Fugas," *De atrásalante en su porfía*, 150.
128. Gelman, "Deslices," *De atrásalante en su porfía*. Buenos Aires: Editorial La Página, 2011, 159.
129. Juan Gelman, "Sí," *Cólera buey. Poesía reunida. Tomo I*. Buenos Aires: Seix Barral, 2012, 173.
130. Juan Gelman, "Dobles," *El emperrado corazón amora*. Buenos Aires: Editorial La Página, 2011, 35.
131. Gelman, "Dobles," 35.
132. Gelman, "Fugas," *El emperrado corazón amora*, 42.
133. Gelman, "Ver si," *El emperrado corazón amora*, 22.
134. Juan Gelman, "Quietos por fin," *Si dulcemente. Interrupciones 1*. Buenos Aires: Editorial La Página, 2011, 162.
135. Gelman, "Quietos por fin," 162.
136. Gelman, "Ya caminando," *Si dulcemente. Interrupciones 1*, 163.
137. Gelman, "Ya caminando," 163.
138. Gelman, "Pensando sus huesitos," *Si dulcemente. Interrupciones 1*, 181.
139. Gelman, "Solísimos," *Si dulcemente. Interrupciones 1*, 167.
140. Juan Gelman, "Aquí," *Hacia el sur. Interrupciones 2*. Buenos Aires: Editorial La Página, 2011, 43.
141. Gelman, "Otras partes," *Hacia el sur. Interrupciones 2*, 50.
142. Juan Gelman, *La junta luz. Poesía reunida. Tomo II*. Buenos Aires: Seix Barral, 2012, 27-30.
143. Juan Gelman, "Notas," *La junta luz. Poesía reunida. Tomo II*, 33.
144. Theodor W. Adorno, *Can One Live After Auschwitz: A Philosophical Reader*. Edited by Rolf Tiedemann, translated by Rodney Livingstone. Stanford: Stanford University Press, 2003.
145. María Esther Gilio, "Juan Gelman habla de su hijo, rescatado de la neblina," *Brecha*. Montevideo, January 19, 1990.
146. The declassified archives of the CIA indicate that Manuel Contreras, chief of DINA (the Chilean secret police) was invited in 1975 to the headquarters of the CIA in Langley, Virginia, for fifteen days. After this visit, Contreras was projected as the "founding inventor" of Plan Condor.

147. Jorge Elías, *Maten al cartero: posdata del asedio a la prensa durante las dictaduras militares del Cono Sur*. Buenos Aires: Fundación Cadal, 2005, 141.
148. Juan Gelman, "Carta abierta a mi nieto o nieta," *Brecha*. Montevideo, Diciembre 23, 1998.
149. Gelman, "Carta abierta a mi nieto o nieta."
150. Gelman, "Carta abierta a mi nieto o nieta."
151. Gelman, "Carta abierta a mi nieto o nieta."
152. Gelman, "Carta abierta a mi nieto o nieta."
153. Gelman, "Carta abierta a mi nieto o nieta."
154. Juan Gelman, open letter published in the newspaper *Página/12* on April 4, 1999, and republished on April 1, 2011, on the life sentence of Eduardo Cabanillas.
155. Gelman, open letter, 1999.
156. Gelman, open letter, 1999.
157. Horacio Verbitsky, "Del amor y la guerra," *Página/12*. Buenos Aires, April 27, 2008.
158. Verbitsky, "Del amor y la guerra," 2008.
159. José Saramago, "Carta abierta de José Saramago a Sanguinetti," *Página/12*. Buenos Aires, October 20, 1999.
160. Saramago, "Carta abierta de José Saramago a Sanguinetti."
161. Saramago, "Carta abierta de José Saramago a Sanguinetti."
162. Saramago, "Carta abierta de José Saramago a Sanguinetti."
163. Gelman, "Carta abierta a mi nieto o nieta."
164. Frente Amplio is an alliance of moderate left parties.
165. Ana Laura Pérez, "Leche envenenada," *Clarín*. Buenos Aires, June 1, 1998.
166. Horacio Verbitsky, "Del amor y la guerra," *Página/12*. Buenos Aires, April 27, 2008.
167. Silvina Friera, "Están reconociendo a un viejísimo amor," *Página/12*. Buenos Aires, November 30, 2007.
168. Juan Gelman, "Cita IV (santa teresa)," *Citas. Interrupciones 1*. Buenos Aires: Editorial La Página, 2011, 266.
169. Gelman, "Cita III (santa teresa)," *Citas. Interrupciones 1*, 265.
170. Gelman, "Cita VIII (santa teresa)," *Citas. Interrupciones 1*, 270.
171. Gelman, "Cita VIII (santa teresa)," *Citas. Interrupciones 1*, 270.
172. Gelman, "Cita VIII (santa teresa)," 270.
173. Gelman, "Cita VIII (santa teresa)," 270.
174. Gelman, "Cita IX (santa teresa)," *Citas. Interrupciones 1*, 271.
175. Gelman, "Cita XLIII (santa teresa)," *Citas. Interrupciones 1*, 297.

176. Gelman uses the neologism "vosmí" in Spanish. Gelman. "Cita XLIII (santa teresa)," 297.
177. Juan Gelman, "I," *Carta abierta. Interrupciones 1*. Buenos Aires: Editorial La Página, 2011, 129.
178. Gelman, "III," *Carta abierta. Interrupciones 1*, 132.
179. Gelman, "III," *Carta abierta. Interrupciones 1*, 132.
180. Gelman, "VI," *Carta abierta. Interrupciones 1*, 135.
181. Gelman, "VIII," *Carta abierta. Interrupciones 1*, 137.
182. Gelman, "XII," *Carta abierta. Interrupciones 1*, 141.
183. Gelman, "XXI," *Carta abierta. Interrupciones 1*, 150.
184. Gelman, "XXV," *Carta abierta. Interrupciones 1*, 154.
185. Rainer Maria Rilke, "La segunda elegía," *Las elegías del Duino, los Réquiem y otros poemas*. Madrid: Visor libros, 2002, 83.
186. Juan Gelman, *De palabra*. Madrid: Editorial Visor, 1994, 7.
187. Gelman, *La junta luz. Poesía reunida. Tomo II*, 13.
188. Gelman, *La junta luz. Poesía reunida. Tomo II*, 38.
189. Gelman, "VII," *Carta abierta. Interrupciones 1*, 136.
190. Gelman, *La junta luz. Poesía reunida. Tomo II*, 13.
191. Gelman, *La junta luz. Poesía reunida. Tomo II*, 13.
192. Gelman, *La junta luz. Poesía reunida. Tomo II,* 14.
193. Gelman, *La junta luz. Poesía reunida. Tomo II,* 14.
194. Gelman, *La junta luz. Poesía reunida. Tomo II*, 14.
195. Gelman, *La junta luz. Poesía reunida. Tomo II*, 51.
196. Gelman, *La junta luz. Poesía reunida. Tomo II*, 51.
197. Juan Gelman, "CCD Automotores Orletti," *Valer la pena*. Buenos Aires: Editorial La Página, 2011, 81.
198. Juan Gelman, "Es," *Mundar*. Buenos Aires: Editorial La Página, 2011, 59.
199. Gelman, "La diosa," *Mundar*, 78.
200. Joaquim Marco. "Mundar. Juan Gelman," *El cultural. El mundo.* Madrid, February 14, 2014.
201. Juan Gelman, "En mí, periodismo y poesía conviven como buenos vecinos," *Página/12, Cultura*. Buenos Aires, April 3, 2002.
202. Juan Gelman, "Heridas y medallas de un poeta," *La Nación*. Buenos Aires, December 10, 1997.
203. Lorenzo Miguel and the Youth Union represented the right-wing faction of the Peronist Movement.
204. Horacio Verbitsky, "Del amor y la guerra," *Página/12*. Buenos Aires, April 27, 2008.

205. Horacio Verbitsky, "La nota de mañana," *Página/12*. Buenos Aires, May 14, 2014.
206. Rogelio García Lupo, "Prosa de Gelman," *La Maga*. No. 28.
207. Verbitsky, "La nota de mañana."
208. Verbitsky, "La nota de mañana."
209. Verbitsky, "La nota de mañana."
210. Silvina Friera, "Su romance con la palabra está al margen de la ideología," *Página/12*. Buenos Aires, December 7, 2014.
211. Adiós a la poesía como arma," *El País*. Madrid, January 15, 2014.
212. "El pibe Juan," *La Maga*. No. 28.
213. Gabriela Esquivada, *Noticias de los Montoneros. La historia del diario que no pudo anunciar la revolución*. Buenos Aires: Editorial Sudamericana, 2005.
214. "El pibe Juan," *La Maga*. No. 28.
215. "El pibe Juan."
216. "El pibe Juan."
217. The quotation refers to the military coup that overthrew the government of Juan Peron in 1955. AA.VV. *El pan duro. Grupo de Poesía*. Buenos Aires: La rosa blindada, 1963.
218. Jorge Boccanera, "Diálogos de Juan," *La Maga*. No. 28, 14.
219. "El pibe Juan."
220. Gelman, "Me batían 'el pibe taquito,'" 73.
221. Preface by Raúl González Tuñón in the first edition of *Violín y otras cuestiones*.
222. Juan Gelman, "Oficio," *Violín y otras cuestiones*. Buenos Aires: Editorial La Página, 2001, 53.
223. Gelman, "Oficio," 53.
224. Enzia Verduchi, "El oficio ardiente," *Brecha*. Montevideo, June 19, 2004.
225. Gelman, "Oficio," 53.
226. Juan Gelman, "Final," *Violín y otras cuestiones*. Buenos Aires: Editorial La Página, 2001, 69.
227. Juan Gelman, "Poema," *El juego en que andamos. Velorio del solo. Gotán*. Buenos Aires: Editorial La Página, 2011, 54.
228. Gelman, "Foto," *El juego en que andamos*, 60.
229. Juan Gelman, "Preguntas," *Cólera buey. Poesía reunida. Tomo I*. Buenos Aires: Seix Barral, 2012, 206.
230. Juan Gelman, "La llave del gas," *Valer la pena*. Buenos Aires: Editorial La Página, 2011, 129.

231. Juan Gelman, "Nota al pie de 'La llave del gas,'" *Valer la pena*. Buenos Aires: Editorial La Página, 2011, 130.
232. Juan Gelman, "¿Qué se sabe?" *Mundar*. Buenos Aires: Editorial La Página, 2011, 88.
233. Gelman, "Final," 69.
234. Juan Gelman, "Operaciones," *Eso. Interrupciones 2*. Buenos Aires: Editorial La Página, 2011, 236. There are interesting similarities between this poem that Gelman wrote in 1986, and the poem written by Billy Collins in 1988 entitled "Introductory to Poetry." "I ask them to take a poem / and hold it up to the light/ like a color slide // or press an ear against its hive. // I say drop a mouse into a poem/ and watch him probe his way out, // or walk inside the poem's room / and feel the walls for a light switch. // I want them to waterski / across the surface of a poem / waving at the author's name on the shore. // But all they want to do / is tie the poem to a chair with rope / and torture a confession out of it. // They begin beating it with a hose / to find out what it really means." In both cases, they highlight deplorable practices of literary criticism.
235. Gelman, "Operaciones," 236.
236. Juan Gelman, "Comentario III (santa teresa)," *Comentarios. Interrupciones 1*. Buenos Aires: Editorial La Página, 2011, 189.
237. Gelman, "Comentario III (santa teresa)," 189.
238. Santa Teresa de Jesús, "Yo toda me entregué y di," *Poesías. Obras Completas*. Madrid: Aguilar, 1945, 719.
239. Santa Teresa de Jesús, "Yo toda me entregué y di," 719.
240. Juan Gelman, "Cita XII (santa teresa)," *Citas. Interrupciones 1*, 274.
241. Gelman, "Cita III (santa teresa)," 265.
242. Gelman, "Cita III (santa teresa)," 265.
243. Juan Gelman, "Cita VI (santa teresa)," *Citas. Interrupciones 1*, 260.
244. Juan Gelman, "en el filo de la belleza que," *Incompletamente*. Buenos Aires: Editorial La Página, 2011, 9.
245. Juan Gelman, "en el filo de la belleza que," 9.
246. Juan Gelman, "Preguntas," *Cólera buey. Poesía reunida. Tomo I*. Buenos Aires: Seix Barral, 2012, 206.
247. Pedro Salvador Ale, "Juan Gelman: la fe poética," *Periódico de Poesía*, No. 11. México, 1995.
248. Juan Gelman, "Exergo," *Com/posiciones. Interrupciones 2*. Buenos Aires: Editorial La Página, 2011, 157.
249. Gelman, "Exergo," 157.

250. Gelman, "Exergo," 157.
251. Gelman, "Exergo," 157.
252. Juan Gelman, "El expulsado," *Com/posiciones. Interrupciones 2*. Buenos Aires: Editorial La Página, 2011, 176.
253. Juan Gelman, "La casa," *Com/posiciones. Interrupciones 2*. Buenos Aires: Editorial La Página, 2011, 181.
254. Juan Gelman, "Los dos llantos," *Com/posiciones. Interrupciones 2*, 201.
255. Juan Gelman, "XXIV," *Dibaxu. Poesía reunida. Tomo II*. Buenos Aires: Seix Barral, 2012, 220.
256. Juan Gelman, "XI," *Dibaxu. Poesía reunida*, 210.
257. Miguel Dalmaroni, "Juan Gelman: las extrañas fronteras del mundo," *Historias que hacen Historia. Psiconet*. Buenos Aires, http://psiconet.com/tiempo/historias/gelman.htm.
258. "El pibe Juan."
259. Daniel García Helder, "Poéticas de la voz. El registro de lo cotidiano," *Historia crítica de la literatura argentina*. Buenos Aires: Emecé, 1999, 214.
260. García Helder, "Poéticas de la voz. El registro de lo cotidiano," 215.
261. Vicente Fidel López, "Tomo VII," *Historia de la República Argentina*. Buenos Aires: Editorial Sopena, 1954, 223.
262. Interview with Enzia Verduchi, "El oficio ardiente," *Brecha*. Montevideo, June 19, 2004.
263. Interview with Enzia Verduchi, "El oficio ardiente," 2004.
264. Juan Gelman, "Lamento por el arbolito de philip," *Los poema de Sidney West*. Buenos Aires: Editorial La Página, 2011, 11.
265. Gelman, "Lamento por la muerte de parsifal hoolig," *Los poema de Sidney West*, 10.
266. Gelman, "Lamento por gallagher bentham," *Los poema de Sidney West*, 15.
267. Gelman, "Lamento por los que envidiaron a david cassidy," *Los poema de Sidney West*, 26.
268. Gelman, "Lamento por el furor de roy hennigan," *Los poema de Sidney West*, 67.
269. Gelman, "Lamento por los idiotas de warren s.w. cormorant," *Los poema de Sidney West*, 69.
270. Gelman, "Lamento por los ojos de vernon vries," *Los poema de Sidney West*, 22.
271. Juan Gelman, "Noticias," *Hacia el sur. Interrupciones 2*. Buenos Aires: Editorial La Página, 2011, 71.

272. Gelman, "Noticias," 115.
273. Gelman, "Verdades," *Hacia el sur. Interrupciones 2*, 117.
274. Gelman, "XII," *Bajo la lluvia ajena (notas al pie de una derrota). Interrupciones 2*, 21.
275. Gelman, "Más preguntas," *Hacia el sur. Interrupciones 2*, 73.
276. Gelman, "Rodolfo dijo que," *Hacia el sur. Interrupciones 2*, 77.
277. Gelman, "Latitud sur," *Hacia el sur. Interrupciones 2*, 75.
278. Marcelo Pichón Rivière, "Una batalla de palabras," *Clarín*. Buenos Aires, September 17, 2000.
279. Horacio Verbitsky, "El universo desnudo," *Página/12*. Buenos Aires, February 2, 2014.
280. Verbitsky, "El universo desnudo," 2014.
281. Juan Gelman, "CXCIV," *Hoy*. Buenos Aires: Seix Barral, 2013, 204.
282. Gelman, "CXLIII," *Hoy*, 246.
283. "Napantla: el pueblo que eligió Juan Gelman para esparcir sus cenizas," *La Nación*. Buenos Aires, January 21, 2014.
284. Juan Gelman, "Paco," *Mundar*. Buenos Aires: Editorial La Página, 2011, 41.
285. Gelman, "Paco," 41.
286. Gelman, "Paco," 41.
287. Gelman, "Volver," *Mundar*, 63.
288. Gelman, "Sucederá," *Mundar*, 44.
289. Gelman, "Canción," *Mundar*, 50.
290. Gelman, "Descubrimiento," *Mundar*, 127.
291. Gelman, "Interrupciones," *Mundar*, 90.
292. Gelman, "El otro," *Mundar*, 109.
293. Verbitsky, "El universo desnudo," 2014.
294. Juan Gelman, "Quien," *De atrásalante en su porfía*. Buenos Aires: Editorial La Página, 2011, 135.
295. Gelman, "Des," *De atrásalante en su porfía*, 56.
296. Gelman, "La gravedad," *De atrásalante en su porfía*, 25.
297. Gelman, "Fugas," *De atrásalante en su porfía*, 150.
298. Gelman, "Teorías," *De atrásalante en su porfía*, 31.
299. Juan Gelman, "LXXXIV," *Hoy*. Buenos Aires: Seix Barral, 2013, 94.
300. Gelman, "LXXXV," *Hoy*, 95.
301. Gelman, "V," *Hoy*, 15.
302. Gelman, "XLII," *Hoy*, 52.
303. Gelman, "XIII," *Hoy*, 23.
304. Gelman, "I," *Hoy*, 11.

305. Gelman, "CCLXI," *Hoy*, 134.
306. Gelman, "CXXIV," *Hoy*, 134.
307. Gelman, "CXXV," *Hoy*, 135.
308. Gelman, "CXXXIII," *Hoy*, 143.
309. Gelman, "IV," *Hoy*, 14.
310. Gelman, "LVI," *Hoy*, 66.
311. Gelman, "LXIV," *Hoy*, 74.
312. Gelman, "LVII," *Hoy*, 67.
313. The author refers to the verses, "siempre se vuelve/ al primer amor" from the tango "Volver" written by Alfredo Le Pera.
314. Res aut ullaboris unto mo dolupta quides dem sum quia videm enemporro molor adi cone nis ex es sam aliquo maios alitios nulpa doluptati nonsequiam hictur apient optur mosseque pero im quam essit, sinus magnit omnimag nihilique nimillaut esequatur susdae nis et omnist, sint enis aliquat endis min cores que mostis doluptat.
315. Asit, simus sequam eria qui ut apis expligenes velenis idelenis eos ea voluptam, optamus moluptate pe dolenih iliberibea cus solupienit lacero tem nonsequatio. Itam rae. Xeris sit elique consequatur? Quid eum suntio dunditae sus.
316. Or sim et dent doluptatem iur apiscillitam andusandiore pliti inullibus nosame prem conseces velit es ipsum id quidi rent, sequos archici untibusda dolorib usapiente quis que quae liciasperiam sum nit repeliqui undigent ut officiis et od esendeb isquis reptatent, omnihic te modion poresci ditibuscias ipsa volupicim dem aut quibusda experes sedi omni cor sit es nobistibus molupta doluptat quaes illest, sollaudiciam fugit lia accaero es etus iducia am vel ium venit qui nestrum aut aboresto magni omni dempore ex et omnisim odiatio nsequi blaborem evelicienis cusdae. Hil et acest, aribusa vel estrunt otaque laut perferferrum abor re velendunt.
317. Ficid quia doloria doluptae nobis eicilitio et, conecta quibus dolorio nsequis restemped qui te volorep taerioria sit destrum eat alia qui occus, to officim ut eum nieturio optatisi qui odiciis incipsae volest imaio experes equiandusa dunt ut omnis nam restotamet, oditas re et quis sit experum con recum fugita veligendit quat exerspitiis ex expelic tem quatur, core pore lit, cus, officaborest aut volo magnimo luptasped quunt omnisincilla volupta corum ut que laborat uscipisque asperro ea duciam fuga. Acest incti natquae od molor re voluptat quossunt quiande consequ ibusam nime quis ipsum eatus as moditia quam de cum volorioremo eum laciisqui ratibus quae qui quas el iumqui as nonse nulparum aut opturepro tor renias

Index

Garcilaso de la Vega, 20, 141

Kreisky, Bruno, 63

Madres de Plaza de Mayo, 90, 106, 179
Mangieri, José Luis, 121, 123, 175, 180
Manzi, Homero, 132
Mao Tse-tung, 122
Marechal, Leopoldo, 21, 45, 66, 192
Martínez, Tomás Eloy, 113, 181
Martino, Francesco de, 63
Mase, Rosario A., 121, 123

About the Author

HERNÁN FONTANET is an Argentinian-Spanish-American author who is intrigued by poetics that emerge in conflict and their potential influence on history. The author of ten volumes on poets and their works, he has served as a professor of literature at Yale, Rider, and North Carolina State Universities and was honored with the 2015 Pakal de Oro award for his groundbreaking work.

Photo by Juan F. Mango